THE BEST INTERESTS OF THE CHILD

Third Edition

Eileen McPartland

BORU

PRESS

Boru Press Ltd
The Farmyard
Birdhill
Co. Tipperary
www.borupress.ie

© Eileen McPartland 2020

ISBN 9781916019959

Print origination by Carole Lynch
Printed by GraphyCems Ltd, Spain

The paper used in this book is made from
wood pulp of managed forests. For every tree felled,
at least one tree is planted, thereby renewing natural
resources.

A CIP catalogue record for this book is available
from the British Library.

CONTENTS

for Seamus

INTRODUCTION

In Ireland, caring for children is a very responsible job: the team of people who look after a child in any setting must ensure that the child's best interests are taken into account in everything that is done in the process of caring for that child. If you are part of a team that is looking after a child, you must learn what is needed to ensure you look after that child's best interests. This principle is enshrined in Irish law and in the individual laws that make up that legislation.

If you work with children in Ireland, you must understand the relevant legislation and keep up to date with changes in that legislation. The reality is that you will be held responsible for your actions if they cause harm to a child. This book introduces the principles of law in relation to childcare and will help you understand how the law affects the care and protection of the children you look after. It explains why you must do certain things and what happens if you do not. It is not intended that you learn every piece of every legal act, but rather that you understand the basics so that you and the children you look after will know what you must and must not do.

The book starts with chapters on the Irish Constitution and the United Nations Convention on the Rights of the Child. These documents are reflected in legislation in relation to the protection and care of children in Ireland and the book highlights their influence.

The book then examines the main pieces of Irish legislation that have an impact on children's lives on a daily basis. It is essential that you know and keep up to date with such legislation.

A glossary also provides explanations of terms and expressions used in the book.

CHAPTER 1

THE IRISH CONSTITUTION

One of the fundamental tools of the legislative system in Ireland is the Irish Constitution *(Bunreacht na hÉireann)*. Among other things, the Constitution sets out the systems and structures of government, the law and the courts, and outlines the rights of citizens. The Constitution can only be amended if a majority of the people of Ireland who are entitled to vote agree to change it in a referendum.

All laws enacted in Ireland must uphold the values and rights set out in the Constitution. To ensure that they do, all acts pass through both Houses of the Oireachtas (the Dáil and the Seanad) before they are signed into law by the President (*Uachtarán na hÉireann*). In some cases the President may first refer the act to either the Supreme Court or what is called the Council of State (a group formed under Article 31 of the Constitution and made up of former taoisigh and some other advisors) for a decision on whether it upholds the fundamental rights outlined in the Constitution.

The Constitution is divided into articles, most of which have paragraphs and sub-paragraphs. Thus, Article 1.1.1° means Article 1, paragraph 1, sub-paragraph 1; Article 22.2.3° means Article 22, paragraph 2, sub-paragraph 3.

If you would like to view the full text of the Constitution, you may download it from www.irishstatutebook.ie or purchase a copy from the Government Publications Office or other bookshops.

Children's rights in Ireland is a complex topic. Much of what is now understood as the legal rights of the child has come about because of long court cases and the deliberations and decisions arising from them. In coming to such decisions, the judge will have had to take into account the best interest of the child in question and what makes most sense in terms of their care.

Children are mentioned in the Constitution under the sections relating to the family (Article 41) and to education (Article 42) and specifically in the new Article 42A, which was added following a referendum of the people and was signed into law on 28 April 2015. In this article, children's rights are acknowledged as being individual.

The Family

Article 41 states:

1   1° The State recognises the Family as the natural primary and fundamental unit group of Society, and as a moral institution possessing inalienable and imprescriptible rights, antecedent and superior to all positive law.

2° The State, therefore, guarantees to protect the Family in its constitution and authority, as the necessary basis of social order and as indispensable to the welfare of the Nation and the State.

2 1° In particular, the State recognises that by her life within the home, woman gives to the State a support without which the common good cannot be achieved.

2° The State shall, therefore, endeavour to ensure that mothers shall not be obliged by economic necessity to engage in labour to the neglect of their duties in the home.

3 1° The State pledges itself to guard with special care the institution of Marriage, on which the Family is founded, and to protect it against attack.

2° A Court designated by law may grant a dissolution of marriage where, but only where, it is satisfied that –

i at the date of the institution of the proceedings, the spouses have lived apart from one another for a period of, or periods amounting to, at least four years during the five years,

ii there is no reasonable prospect of a reconciliation between the spouses, iii such provision as the Court considers proper having regard to the circumstances exists or will be made for the spouses, any children of either or both of them and any other person prescribed by law, and

iv any further conditions prescribed by law are complied with.

3° No person whose marriage has been dissolved under the civil law of any other State but is a subsisting valid marriage under the law for the time being in force within the jurisdiction of the Government and Parliament established by this Constitution shall be capable of contracting a valid marriage within that jurisdiction during the lifetime of the other party to the marriage so dissolved.

4° Marriage may be contracted in accordance with law by two persons without distinction as to their sex.

It is interesting to note that Article 41 mentions the family rather than the child and therefore the main protections within that Article of Constitution are afforded to the family and not to the individual child unless, as already explained, they are established by court cases. This goes some way to explain the method of justice in the Irish legal system where children are represented in court by their family until they reach the age of eighteen (the age at which they are deemed to be adults) and gain their rights as an adult.

The final part of this article (4°), was added as a result of the 34th Amendment of the Constitution (Marriage Equality Act 2015), the aim of which was to reflect a more modern Ireland where marriage may not be of the traditional husband–wife composition. This amendment ensures that different family types are legally recognised, regardless of whether parents are married, as long as their relationship is within the law. This covers same-sex parents and their children as well as other family types and ensures that children of these family compositions are not denied any legal protections just because their parents are not husband and wife, as was the case before the referendum was passed.

One of the relevant points in this scenario is that while there is usually a time limit within which a person can take a civil case against another for some harm done, the situation is different in the case of a child. In practice, the family can take a case in such situations within the time period from the time of the wrong done to the child, but where the family does not take such a case, the child can do so within that time period *after* reaching the age of majority (eighteen). In other words, the child has until the age of eighteen plus the required time to take a case. This limit may be extended to an even older age in special or what are called extenuating circumstances, perhaps based on capacity to take a case or indeed the level of knowledge of the harm done. This point has been the subject of Supreme Court cases and it is not possible to go into the complicated details of these in this book.

Education

Article 42 states:

1   The State acknowledges that the primary and natural educator of the child is the Family and guarantees to respect the inalienable right and duty of parents to provide, according to their means, for the religious and moral, intellectual, physical and social education of their children.

2   Parents shall be free to provide this education in their homes or in private schools or in schools recognised or established by the State.

1° The State shall not oblige parents in violation of their conscience and lawful preference to send their children to schools established by the State, or to any particular type of school designated by the State.

2° The State shall, however, as guardian of the common good, require in view of actual conditions that the children receive a certain minimum education, moral, intellectual and social.

3 The State shall provide for free primary education and shall endeavour to supplement and give reasonable aid to private and corporate educational initiative, and, when the public good requires it, provide other educational facilities or institutions with due regard, however, for the rights of parents, especially in the matter of religious and moral formation.

You will notice that Article 41 mentions the 'natural and imprescriptible rights of the child' and Article 42 refers to the 'duty' of parents towards their children. However, there is no discussion of what precisely the rights of a child are or what constitutes a parent's duty. Such anomalies or unexplained differences exist in many legal documents, which are often left open for interpretation by the courts. While some may see the lack of detail in relation to the rights of the child as a problem, others consider it a strength because when you state specific rights you limit those rights to what exactly is stated. In the Constitution this limit does not exist and so the protection of children is all-encompassing.

Another anomaly in the Constitution, and found in Article 42, revolves around the expression 'right and duty', two terms which are often grouped together without distinguishing one from the other. This expression may stem from the fact that the Constitution was originally worded in Irish and the Irish word *duchas* may, in some areas, be used to describe both a right and a duty. Remembering that in any question on the Constitution the Irish version prevails, this makes it almost impossible to say whether 'right' or 'duty' was the original meaning intended, in which case both may be used together.

The phrase 'imprescriptible rights' refers to rights that cannot be removed just because you ignore them or do not use them. In other words, whether you choose to use them daily, occasionally or never choose to exercise them, these rights cannot be taken away from you. 'Inalienable' rights means that they belong to you alone and cannot be sold or transferred to another person.

The newly inserted Article 42A, as discussed earlier, was passed in what was called the Children Referendum 2012, which meant that for the first time ever, children in Ireland have a specific section of our Constitution that relates to them. Article 42A states:

1   The State recognises and affirms the natural and imprescriptible rights of all children and shall, as far as practicable, by its laws protect and vindicate those rights.

2   1° In exceptional cases, where the parents, regardless of their marital status, fail in their duty towards their children to such extent that the safety and welfare of any of their children is likely to be prejudicially affected the State as guardian of the common good shall, by proportionate means as provided by law, endeavour to supply the

place of the parents, but always with due regard for the natural and imprescriptible rights of the child.

2° Provision shall be made by law for the adoption of any child where the parents have failed for such a period of time as may be prescribed by law in their duty towards the child and where the best interests of the child so require.

3   Provision shall be made by law for the voluntary placement for adoption and the adoption of any child.

4   1° Provision shall be made by law that in the resolution of all proceedings –

i   brought by the State, as guardian of the common good, for the purpose of preventing the safety and welfare of any child from being prejudicially affected, or

ii concerning the adoption, guardianship or custody of, or access to, any child, the best interests of the child shall be the paramount consideration.

2° Provision shall be made by law for securing, as far as practicable, that in all proceedings referred to in subsection 1° of this section in respect of any child who is capable of forming his or her own views, the views of the child shall be ascertained

> and given due weight having regard to the age and maturity of the child.

The Article above, while new, does have some aspects to it which have not yet been seen in operation in any court cases, and it is a departure from the original wording of the protections for the child within the Family in Article 41. Notably, Section 1 above does not state that the rights being given to the child are 'inalienable' as was used in Article 41. This is particularly significant as the views of the child will be 'given due weight having regard to the age and maturity of the child'. It may seem as if the child's age and level of maturity might affect the exact protections and support being given to the child and this may well be the subject of legal query in the future.

Additionally Article 42A states that the State shall 'as far as practicable by its laws protect and vindicate those rights'. This is not the same as the wording in Article 41, where the State 'guarantees to protect'. The use of the word 'practicable' is effectively interpreted as allowing for cost, practical or other considerations to be taken into account in making a decision as to whether the action of the State in supporting the child would be reasonable to implement. It is not a fully unconditional promise or undertaking to fight for the rights of the child, and so leaves lots of potential 'wriggle room' and falls short of an unconditional guarantee. This may have significance when we see this Article being contested in court cases in the future, when the exact application of the meaning will be given more defined shape by judges.

Article 42A also introduces the notion that children can be voluntarily considered for or given up for adoption by their parents, which is a very raw issue in Ireland where children were given up for adoption in contentious circumstances as outlined in the Ryan Report on Child Abuse in Ireland. Now the possibility is open to all parents 'regardless of their marital status' (meaning whether they are married or not). Ireland has many children in the care or foster system as *legally* both parents had to agree together to give a child up for adoption, and where this could not be agreed, the children usually ended up in the limbo of foster homes for perhaps the entirety of their childhood. Article 42A should make a difference to this situation as it tries to ensure that the previous obstacle of permission can be overcome. This would obviously be in a child's best interests as the child can then have the permanency of a home.

Another perhaps more fundamental change brought about by Article 42A is the potential for children to be taken away from parents who fail to provide for them for a specific time. The Article states that the time can be set by law and therefore at any stage the time limit can be changed by altering the legislation passed. This allows not just one child but possibly all the children in a family to be adopted to protect their best interests. This time limit has not been set out yet; however, there is a potential that if, for instance, a parent is sent to jail, upon their release they might discover that, in the best interests of the children, those children have been adopted by others.

There are other reasons besides incarceration as to why a parent may be deemed incapable of providing for their child's welfare and best interests. In many of those cases, the option of adoption may offer the child a very different future, which may be in the child's best interests.

Throughout Article 42A it is obvious that the child is the paramount consideration in the issues that might arise. Specifically the Article outlines that in any proceedings brought by the State concerning the changes that might arise in a child's life as a result of the Article, the views and opinions of the child or children individually must 'be ascertained and given due weight having regard to the age and maturity of the child'. The views of the child are however not guaranteed to result in any changes taking place in the planned adoption of the child but must merely be listened to, as there is no exact definition of what 'due weight' implies.

Fundamental to any discussion on the new Article 42A is the concept that the rights protected will be based in law and not specified in the Constitution. Laws can be changed by politicians without any referral back to the people for their approval, while constitutional protections can only be changed by agreement of a majority of the population who vote at referendum.

CHAPTER 2

UN CONVENTION ON THE RIGHTS OF THE CHILD

In 1989 world leaders got together to draw up a legally binding agreement to protect children, recognising that children are a vulnerable part of society. The result was the United Nations (UN) Convention on the Rights of the Child, which sets out those rights in fifty-four articles and two optional protocols. The text of the Convention is reproduced in Appendix 1 of this book.

The Convention is not a piece of legislation in itself but it has shaped laws that have been passed since 1989 in Ireland and in other countries in relation to the care and welfare of children. Conventions are ratified (accepted and agreed to) by countries who accept their basic principals and agree to incorporate their ideals into the laws of that country.

In essence, the Convention on the Rights of the Child states that children have basic human rights: to survival; to develop to their fullest potential; to protection from harmful influences, abuse and exploitation; and to participate fully in family, cultural and social life. This chapter highlights some of the key sections of the Convention.

Core Principles

The four core principles of the Convention are:

- Non-discrimination
- Devotion to the best interests of the child
- The right to life, survival and development
- Respect for the views of the child.

It is important to remember these core principles when looking at legislation that has been passed in countries that have ratified the Convention. Such countries have committed to these principles and you will see these expressions used in their laws.

Ireland has incorporated many aspects of the Convention into its laws and the four core principles are evident in the words and ideals of Irish legislation in relation to children. One of the main acts of law passed in Ireland since ratifying the Convention is the Child Care Act 1991, which has clearly adopted these core values and in whose text the above expressions can be found.

Preamble

The Preamble reminds us that the United Nations states in the Universal Declaration of Human Rights that 'childhood is entitled to special care and assistance' and also recognises the family 'as the fundamental group of society' (just as the Irish Constitution did in 1937). It stresses the ideal that children should be cared for and protected until they are in a position to lead an 'individual life in society'. Not surprisingly, the ideals of the Convention on the Rights of the Child sit easily alongside Irish laws.

Article 1

Article 1 sets out the definition of a child as someone under the age of eighteen unless otherwise defined in the laws of an individual country.

In the case of Ireland, the Disability Act 2005 sets the age at eighteen, as does the Child Care Act 1991. The Disability Act 2005 goes further by saying that a person with a disability of such an extent that the person cannot live an independent life without support is entitled to the protections of a child under the act. The act defines a disability as follows:

> 'Disability', in relation to a person, means a substantial restriction in the capacity of the person to carry on a profession, business or occupation in the State or to participate in social or cultural life in the State by reason of an enduring physical, sensory, mental health or intellectual impairment.

The act explains the term 'substantial restriction' in relation to a disability as something that:

(a)   is permanent or likely to be permanent, results in a significant difficulty in communication, learning or mobility or in significantly disordered cognitive processes, and

(b)   gives rise to the need for services to be provided continually to the person whether or not a child or, if the person is a child, to the need for services to be provided early in life to ameliorate the disability.

The age at which a person is no longer a child in relation to the legal system in Ireland is eighteen, except in the case of disability where it could be older than eighteen. It is not a clear cut-off at eighteen, and as a person working with children you need to ensure that you apply this distinction. You cannot assume that the person in front of you has the capacity to understand the implications of some decisions you may require that person to make. Depending on the capacity (ability to understand the significance of the issue) of the person in the situation, you may need to seek the agreement of parents or people besides yourself who also act *in loco parentis* (in the place of parents) for some issues that may arise, even if the person is over eighteen years of age.

Article 2

Article 2 seeks to protect children from discrimination on grounds similar to the nine grounds now stated under Ireland's Equal Status Acts 2000 to 2004. It specifically states that children should not be discriminated against or punished on the basis of the actions, beliefs or stated opinions of their parents, legal guardians or family members. This article has the potential to have far-reaching implications.

Article 3

Every person working with children should note this article. It is one of the most fundamental aspects of the Convention as it states that the primary consideration in relation to a child will be 'the best interests of the child'. This is the most important aspect of good practice in relation to the care of children in Ireland. The Child Care Act 1991 and subsequent acts are all concerned with promoting 'the best interests of the child'.

Article 3 also states that children should be cared for by competent people in suitable situations that meet set supervisory standards. This has relevance to the process of National Vetting in Ireland for people working with children. The suitability of staff, institutions, services and facilities are the duty of States parties that have adopted the Convention and this includes suitability and competence in relation to training and understanding the needs of the children in your care as well as being proven not to be a potential threat yourself to the children in your care.

The fundamentals of Irish rules for childcare facilities are set out in the childcare regulations Child Care Act 1991 (Early Years Services) Regulations 2016 and the very recent Child Care Act 1991 (Early Years Services) (Registration of School Age Services) Regulations 2018. The 2016 regulations set out such things as the minimum carer/child ratios and space provisions required for any pre-school facility in Ireland, while the 2018 regulations deal with services who cater for school-age children. Such services are required since 18 February 2019 (the date of commencement) to register with Tusla. These limits ensure that the child's safety and welfare is taken into account. In relation to other care situations, stipulations in various relevant acts describe 'recognised' or 'approved' centres that are over-seen by the State, which is charged with ensuring the suitability of such establishments under this article of the Convention.

The protection of the best interests of the child is a fundamental undertaking of any childcare worker. It should be the case that every childcare worker knows what is in the best interests of the children in their care, but it is also important to note that **unless** the child is allowed to express their opinions on the matter, in line with their own level of maturity and understanding, then what is in the best interests of individual children is open to interpretation by adults who legislate on behalf of children, whether in the role of parent or *in loco parentis*. The child has a fundamental right to be included in the process if they have the capacity to understand and contribute to the decision-making process.

Article 5

This article states that parents have 'rights and duties' and it extends these duties to people who are in the place of parents (*in loco parentis*) for whatever reason. As with the Irish Constitution, the concepts of rights and duties are mentioned together in this article. The duty appears to be owed to the child in the case of the Convention. The Convention recognises that these rights and duties will change over time depending on 'the evolving capacities of the child'.

Articles 9, 19 and 25

Article 9 goes a little further in relation to the concept that a duty is owed to a child. It states that children should receive assistance from the State to contact their parent(s) when they have been separated – this might mean being in contact with parents who live in different countries and other certain circumstances – *except* where it is not in the best interests of the child to do so.

This principle has been incorporated into the Protection of Children (Hague Convention) Act 2000, which deals with issues such as the concept of jurisdiction, enforcement of parental rights, co-operation in relation to the protection of children and repatriation of children who have been abducted. The act allows orders to be made by a District Court judge in relation to a parent seeking access to his or her child. In this aim, the District Court judge may exercise the jurisdiction of either the District or Circuit Court in emergency situations to decide in the best interests of the child if one parent qualifies for access.

Article 19 endorses the use of educational measures (such as parenting or counselling courses) to protect the child from abuse, negligence, maltreatment or exploitation while in the care of parents or others, *in loco parentis*, which would also include social programmes of support for the child and those charged with the child's care. This stance is based on the conviction stated in the Preamble that 'the family, as the fundamental group of society and the natural environment for the growth and well-being of all its members and particularly children, should be afforded the necessary protection and assistance so that it can fully assume its responsibilities within the community'.

Article 25 recognises the right of a child in the care of a competent authority to have that care provision reviewed periodically. This right will be discussed further when we examine the Mental Health Act 2001.

These articles form the basis of Ireland's child protection provisions in the Child Care Act 1991, where the goal is clearly stated as being the best interests of the child. To this end, the protection of the child is stated as being in a family situation except in cases where such a situation is not in the child's best interests.

Article 12

Article 12 gives children the right to form their own opinions and views and to express them. This right has been evident in Ireland in the selection pro-cess for the post of Ombudsman for Children, which involved children in choosing the best candidate for the job. Indeed the ongoing work of the Ombudsman's Office continues to invite the opinions of children in relation to their lives and experiences.

The article goes even further by stating that a child has a right to representation in judicial or administrative proceedings in relation to that child. Ireland has sought to include these ideals in legislation, specifically in the Child Care Act 1991, and they have now also been included in Article 42A of the Constitution as agreed to by the majority of people who voted by referendum.

Article 23

This article deals with disabled children and their right to inclusion, full participation and effective access to and participation 'in a manner conducive to the child's achieving the fullest possible social integration and individual development, including his or her cultural and spiritual development'. This goal also underpins Ireland's Education for Persons with Special Educational Needs Act 2004 and Disability Act 2005. The more recently adopted (ratified March 2018) UN Convention on the Rights of Persons with a Disability (CRPD) also clearly underpins the idea in relation to children and those with a disability particularly in relation to inclusion and reasonable assistance to achieve goals set.

Article 28

Article 28 forms the basis of Ireland's Educational (Welfare) Act 2004 from the point of view of putting in place measures to ensure school attendance and reducing drop-out rates.

Article 31

Article 31 sets out the rights of children to play, recreation, artistic expression and participation in culture. Every person who works with children must ensure that the rights of children are adhered to within their work, and this right to play, recreation and artistic expression as well as participation in culture can direct some of the work done with children. Every crèche, school, playgroup and other child-centred facility must ensure that these elements are covered in its daily routines as children today often spend as much time there as they do with their parents.

———

Ireland ratified the UN Convention on the Rights of the Child, and in so doing undertook to implement its provisions into Irish laws made after the ratification date. The first major piece of legislation following the ratification date was the Child Care Act 1991, which replaced the dated Children's Act 1908 (which itself pre-dated the Irish Constitution).

CHAPTER 3

THE CHILD CARE ACT 1991

The Child Care Act 1991 is very important in relation to the protection of children. It was enacted after the UN Convention on the Rights of the Child and the ideals of the Convention can be recognised in the wording of the act, including use of the expression 'the best interests of the child'. The act puts a legal responsibility on any person charged with the care of any child to act in the child's best interests – this is the most fundamental requirement of every person who works with children in whatever situation.

The act as originally written defines a child as a person under the age of eighteen, except someone who is or has been married, but this exclusion specifically used in the 1991 act has been modified since, as already explained in the discussion above on the Disability Act 2005.

The act is divided into ten parts, some of which are administrative. This chapter outlines the key parts of the act, which any person working in childcare or any student of childcare **must** know and understand.

Part II

This part charges the health boards, then the Health Service Executive (HSE), with the welfare of children in their region and provides for the establishment of childcare advisory committees in each health service area. This responsibility has since been transferred to the Child and Family Agency (Tusla), which was provided for by the Child and Family Agency Act 2013.

Part III

Part III allows for Gardaí to remove a child from a situation of immediate danger and to make an emergency care order in relation to that child. It recognises that the best place for a child is with the family, as provided for in the Constitution and indeed in the Convention on the Rights of the Child, but acknowledges that sometimes a child is in immediate danger with the family and must be taken elsewhere.

Part IV

This part underlines Ireland's commitment to the principles of the Convention on the Rights of the Child in so far as there is a legal requirement to go to court to review emergency care orders. It also allows for interim care orders, legally enforceable care orders and supervision orders with judicial review of decisions made on behalf of the child in question.

Part V

Part V allows for a child to receive legal representation in relation to the orders by allowing for the appointment by the court of a solicitor and guardian *ad litem* (who represents the best interests of the child) and provides that the privacy of the child be protected and the child's welfare prioritised.

Part VI

Children can be placed in foster care or residential care or some family care that is in their best interests. This part also provides for periodic reviews and supervision as outlined in the Convention on the Rights of the Child.

Part VII

Part VII relates to what childcare workers need to know in order to do their job properly, thus fulfilling the requirement in the Convention on the Rights of the Child for the child to be cared for in a competent institution.

This part also provides for childcare regulations to underpin the operation of childcare facilities, including stating the space requirements for every child in a setting and the carer/child ratios. It is important to note that the actual regulations are not contained in the Child Care Act 1991, thus avoiding the need to amend the whole act every time a change is made to the regulations. The regulations are separate and are updated from time to time to take account of changes in policy in relation to the operation of child-centred facilities.

Part VIII

This part provides for the registration, staffing, services and facilities of residential centres.

———

Despite the introduction of the Child Care Act 1991, which is the definitive act in relation to child protection in Ireland, people still remain reluctant, for fear of repercussions, to make a report of abuse that might result in a child being removed from a family. This reluctance limited the effectiveness of the act and necessitated the passing of further legislation, namely the Protection for Persons Reporting Child Abuse Act 1998.

Additionally, the reluctance to report abuse for any personal reasons meant that children were not adequately protected and it was necessary to make people legally responsible if they do not report abuse. This has been done by ensuring that, in some jobs, people have a duty to report abuse, making those jobs ones where mandatory reporting is required. Childcare or a job specifically working with children is such a job. This means that you, as a person working in childcare or directly with children, have no choice but to report abuse if you become aware of it in relation to the children you work with. You are what is now called a **mandated person**.

CHAPTER 4

PROTECTION FOR PERSONS REPORTING CHILD ABUSE ACT 1998

The Protection for Persons Reporting Child Abuse Act 1998 provides immunity from being sued for damages for people who report suspicions of abuse 'reasonably and in good faith' to designated health service staff or the Gardaí. It also protects employees from being discriminated against or sacked because they may have made a report of child abuse 'reasonably and in good faith'. The act was updated in October 2015 to keep it in line with more recent legislation but the original name still applies. This act is fundamental to the effectiveness of the Child Care Act 1991 as, prior to its passing, people were afraid of being sued when they reported a suspicion of child abuse.

The act states that a suspicion of abuse consists of an opinion that:

(a) a child has been or is being assaulted, ill-treated, neglected or sexually abused, or

(b) a child's health, development or welfare has been or is being avoidably impaired or neglected

The act has no protection for somebody who makes a false allegation 'knowing' the statement made to be 'false'; indeed, it provides for prosecution on criminal charges in such cases. This measure protects people from malicious acts in relation to child abuse reporting.

The act has also been amended in relation to a communication deemed to be a 'protected disclosure' under the Protected Disclosures Act 2014, which is not directly aimed at situations of childcare, although it might affect a childcare situation. This is a specific legal process not covered in this book.

Importantly, the act is not about mandatory reporting of suspicions of abuse; its aim is rather to protect those who do report their suspicions. It does not protect a person who reports a suspicion from threats and intimidation in their everyday life, however, and this may be a failing in the act as in some societal situations intimidation following a disclosure can become a part of everyday life for people. However, the care of children and the protection of their best interests should never be taken lightly, and children by their very nature require adults and people in positions of responsibility towards them to take that care very seriously and to ensure the child's care, welfare and best interests take precedence.

Role of Childcare Worker

The year 1999 saw the publication of *Children First: National Guidelines for the Protection and Welfare of Children*. That publication has since been updated as a result of the Children First Act 2015, and together these documents set out the very detailed procedures to be followed by organisations in relation to child protection and define the different forms of abuse in concise terms (see Chapter 5). Every worker or student working with children should be familiar with these definitions as part of their work skills.

The guidelines require you to be vigilant in your work and to note things that you observe in relation to the children in your care. The observation methods you learn as a student will be the ones you use in relation to child protection and you should be confident that the observations you make can be used as part of a body of evidence in a child protection situation should that prove necessary. This explains why recording of child observations, which is done as part and parcel of your work in any childcare capacity, should be properly and professionally carried out, why it is important to protect the integrity of the information recorded and why you should at all times be very diligent in relation to your observations.

To this end, the importance of keeping a reflective diary in relation to working in any setting that involves the care and support of children cannot be overstated. Only by reflection can you put in context what you see and how you carry out your work with children. It is a process that changes continually as the child develops within your care, and contemporaneous notes (those made as you go along) can form the basis of a child's protection where you may have noticed that things do not seem right.

Always remember:

Working in childcare is a team effort and all members work together in the best interests of the child.

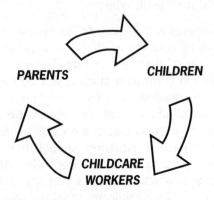

PARENTS   **CHILDREN**

CHILDCARE WORKERS

Anybody working with children should be proud to be part of the care contract that seeks to ensure that the child's best interests are met. It requires you to always consider how your actions impact on the child in your care and how best that impact should be directed to ensure that the child gets the most out of your interaction together, bearing in mind the child's age, stage of development and evolving capacities.

While observation is hugely important in this process, discipline, professionalism, insight, trust, mutual respect and consideration are also fundamental concepts in your working relationship with children as well as the ability to predict the needs of a child in any given situation.

The *National Guidance for the Protection and Welfare of Children,* published by the Department of Children and Youth Affairs in 2017, outlines some very relevant principles on which the protection of children are based and should provide guidance for how this topic is approached:

- The safety and welfare of children is everyone's responsibility.
- The best interests of the child should be paramount.
- The overall aim in all dealings with children and their families is to intervene proportionately to support families to keep children safe from harm.
- Interventions by the State should build on existing strengths and protective factors in the family.
- Early intervention is key to getting better outcomes. Where it is necessary for the State to intervene to keep children safe, the minimum intervention necessary should be used.
- Children should only be separated from parents/ guardians when alternative means of protecting them have been exhausted.
- Children have a right to be heard, listened to and taken seriously. Taking account of their age and understanding, they should be consulted

and involved in all matters and decisions that may affect their lives.

- Parents/guardians have a right to respect, and should be consulted and involved in matters that concern their family.

- A proper balance must be struck between protecting children and respecting the rights and needs of parents/guardians and families. Where there is conflict, the child's welfare must come first.

- Child protection is a multiagency, multi-disciplinary activity. Agencies and professionals must work together in the interests of children.

Everybody should be aware of the overall goals of these statements and they should be applied whenever anybody works or interacts with children. In this way the whole process becomes second nature to everybody and each child can be enabled to have a life that is rewarding and full of promise.

CHAPTER 5

DEFINITIONS OF ABUSE

This chapter is based around extracts from *Children First: National Guidance for the Protection and Welfare of Children* (2017), which is based on the Children First Act 2015. Therefore, the information provided is reflective of the actual descriptions and instructions contained in that guidance document. It is also important to remember that only social workers are in a position to progress any type of investigation into an allegation of suspected child abuse. It is not the job of people who work in childcare, for instance, to start any investigation, as their role is only to report any suspicions they may have so that they can be forwarded correctly.

The Children First Act 2015 as the guidance document (2017) sets out to:

- Raise awareness of child abuse and neglect
- Provide for mandatory reporting by key professionals
- Improve child safeguarding arrangements in organisations providing services to children
- Provide for co-operation and information-sharing between agencies when Tusla is undertaking child protection assessments.

Note that the definition of a child in the 2017 guidance document is stated as meaning a person under the age of eighteen years who is not or has not been married.

Signs and Symptoms of Child Neglect

Child neglect is the most common category of abuse. A distinction can be made between 'wilful' neglect and 'circumstantial' neglect. 'Wilful' neglect would generally incorporate a direct and deliberate deprivation by a parent or a carer of a child's most basic needs (such as withdrawal of food, shelter, warmth, clothing and contact with others). 'Circumstantial' neglect more often may be due to stress or an inability of parents/carers to cope.

The guidance document points out that neglect is associated with poverty but is not necessarily caused by it. It may also be related to parental incapacity due to learning disability or psychological disturbance. The guidance document outlines that child neglect is the most frequently reported category of abuse, both in Ireland and internationally, and that ongoing neglect may have serious long-term negative consequences for children. What is important in this outline is that there should be no judgement of any person in relation to neglect until all the facts of a case are known. This can only happen when the properly qualified people investigate all the facts and use their expertise to make such a judgement.

The neglect of children may often be about not doing enough for the child, which can lead to the child not developing to the best of their ability, be it emotionally, physically or cognitively.

Child neglect should be suspected in cases of:

- Abandonment or desertion
- Children persistently being left alone without adequate care and supervision
- Malnourishment, lack of food, inappropriate food or erratic feeding
- Lack of warmth and adequate clothing
- Lack of protection and exposure to danger including moral danger or lack of supervision appropriate to the child's age
- Persistent failure to attend school
- Non-organic failure to thrive, for example a child failing to gain weight not only because of malnutrition but also due to emotional deprivation
- Failure to provide adequate care for the child's medical and development needs, including intellectual stimulation
- Exploitation or overworking.

Signs and Symptoms of Emotional Child Abuse

The guidance document outlines that emotional abuse is the systematic emotional or psychological ill-treatment of a child as part of the overall relationship between a caregiver and a child.

Emotional abuse occurs when adults responsible for taking care of children are unable to be aware of and unable (for a range of reasons) to meet the child's emotional and developmental needs. The guidance document specifically outlines that no one indicator is conclusive evidence of emotional abuse and that emotional abuse is not easy to recognise because the effects are not easily observable.

Emotional abuse can be seen in some specific ways as pointed out by the guidance document:

- Rejection
- Lack of comfort and love
- Lack of attachment
- Lack of proper stimulation (e.g. fun and play)
- Continuous lack of praise and encouragement
- Persistent criticism, sarcasm, hostility or blaming of the child
- Lack of continuity of care (e.g. frequent moves, particularly unplanned)
- Serious over-protectiveness
- Conditional parenting in which care for or affection of a child depends on his or her behaviour or actions
- Inappropriate non-physical punishment (e.g. locking children in bedrooms)
- Ongoing family conflicts and/or family violence
- Seriously inappropriate expectations of a child relative to his or her age and stage of development which impacts on the child negatively.

It is very important for those who work with children to note that no one indicator is conclusive of emotional abuse, and a child shows signs of emotional abuse through their actions or emotions in several ways as outlined in the guidance document. These indicators would include insecure attachment, unhappiness, low self-esteem, educational and developmental underachievement, risk taking and aggressive behaviour. The child themselves may not be aware that their actions are caused by emotional abuse as they may not fully grasp the situation, but often adults can spot them. That is why it is important to observe patterns and not necessarily one-off instances.

Signs and Symptoms of Physical Child Abuse

One of the first things to note in relation to the concept of physical abuse is the fact that the Children First Act 2015 abolished the legal defence of what was called reasonable chastisement in court cases, which therefore meant that people cannot claim that when they hit a child, it is reasonable chastisement. Therefore, the hitting of a child is deemed to be assault just as it would be in relation to an adult being hit.

Physical abuse is, as the guidance document points out, when someone deliberately hurts a child physically or puts them at risk of being physically hurt either in a single incident or as a pattern of incidents. Physical abuse can include the following as set out in the guidance document:

- Physical punishment
- Beating, slapping, hitting or kicking
- Pushing, shaking or throwing
- Pinching, biting, choking or hair pulling
- Use of excessive force in handling
- Deliberate poisoning
- Suffocation
- Fabricated or induced illness
- Female genital mutilation.

There are many different forms of physical abuse but skin, mouth and bone injuries are the most common.

Signs and Symptoms of Sexual Child Abuse

Sexual child abuse often covers a wide number of abusive activities. It rarely involves just a single incident and can occur over a number of years. Sexual child abuse frequently happens within the family, and can include older siblings and extended family members, but is not confined to family situations. The fact that the child does not understand what sexual activity is and therefore does not understand that it is a form of abuse, cannot mean that it does not amount to sexual abuse – in other words the innocence of the child is no defence for the abuser. The guidance document outlines some examples of what constitutes sexual abuse as follows:

- Any sexual act intentionally performed in the presence of a child
- An invitation to sexual touching or intentional touching or molesting of a child's body whether by a person or object for the purpose of sexual arousal or gratification
- Masturbation in the presence of a child or the involvement of a child in an act of masturbation
- Sexual intercourse with a child, whether oral, vaginal or anal
- Sexual exploitation of a child which includes:

  Inviting, inducing or coercing a child to engage in prostitution or the production of child pornography (for example, exhibition, modelling or posing for the purpose of sexual arousal, gratification or sexual act, including its recording [on film, videotape or other media] or the manipulation, for those purposes, of an image by computer or other means)

  - Inviting, coercing or inducing a child to participate in, or to observe, any sexual, indecent or obscene act

  - Showing sexually explicit material to children which is often a feature of the 'grooming' process by perpetrators of abuse

- Exposing a child to inappropriate or abusive material through information and communication technology

- Consensual sexual activity involving an adult with an underage person. In relation to child sexual abuse, the guidance document notes that, for the purposes of the criminal law, the age of consent for sexual intercourse is seventeen years for both boys and girls. It points out that any sexual relationship where one or both parties are under the age of seventeen is illegal but that such sexual relationship may not necessarily be regarded as sexual abuse.

Gardaí will conduct the criminal investigation into allegations of sexual abuse as that is within their responsibilities to protect children from harm.

Behavioural Signs

In relation to instances of sexual abuse, some of the following behavioural signs may be evident and may alert a person working with children that something may be going on:

- Noticeable and uncharacteristic change of behaviour
- Hints about sexual activity
- Age-inappropriate understanding of sexual behaviour
- Inappropriate seductive behaviour
- Sexually aggressive behaviour with others
- Uncharacteristic sexual play with peers or toys
- Unusual reluctance to join in normal activities that involve undressing (e.g. games/swimming).

Where such signs are evident, it may be justification for bringing reasonable concerns to the attention of Tusla for investigation.

The guidance document sets out a list that may help those working with children to identify a range of issues in a child's life that may place them at greater risk of abuse or neglect while pointing out that the presence of those factors do not necessarily mean that in those circumstances or settings a child is being abused. This list is included in Appendix 2.

The Criminal Law (Sexual Offences) Act 2017, as outlined in the guidance document, was specifically enacted to address the sexual exploitation of children and targets those who engage in this criminal activity. It creates offences relating to the obtaining or providing of children for the purposes of sexual exploitation. It also creates offences of the types of activity that may occur during the early stages of the predatory process prior to the actual exploitation of a child, for example, using modern technology to prey on children and making arrangements to meet with a child where the intention is to sexually exploit the child.

Bullying as a Form of Abuse

This is a very important aspect of the protection of children and the guidance document clearly outlines the issues in relation to bullying as follows:

> It is recognised that bullying affects the lives of an increasing number of children and can

be the cause of genuine concerns about a child's welfare.

Bullying can be defined as repeated aggression – whether it is verbal, psychological or physical – that is conducted by an individual or group against others. It is behaviour that is intentionally aggravating and intimidating, and occurs mainly among children in social environments such as schools. It includes behaviours such as physical aggression, cyber-bullying, damage to property, intimidation, isolation/exclusion, name calling, malicious gossip and extortion. Bullying can also take the form of abuse based on gender identity, sexual preference, race, ethnicity and religious factors. With developments in modern technology, children can also be the victims of non-contact bullying, via mobile phones, the internet and other personal devices.

While bullying can happen to any child, some may be more vulnerable. These include: children with disabilities or special educational needs; those from ethnic minority and migrant groups; from the Traveller community; lesbian, gay, bisexual or transgender (LGBT) children and those perceived to be LGBT; and children of minority religious faiths.

There can be an increased vulnerability to bullying among children with special educational needs. This is particularly so among those who do not understand social cues and/

or have difficulty communicating. Some children with complex needs may lack understanding of social situations and therefore trust everyone implicitly. Such children may be more vulnerable because they do not have the same social skills or capacity as others to recognise and defend themselves against bullying behaviour.

Bullying in schools is a particular problem due to the fact that children spend a significant portion of their time there and are in large social groups. In the first instance, the school authorities are responsible for dealing with such bullying. School management boards must have a code of behaviour and an anti-bullying policy in place. If you are a staff member of a school, you should also be aware of your school's anti-bullying policy and of the relevant guidelines on how it is handled.

In cases of serious instances of bullying where the behaviour is regarded as possibly abusive, you may need to make a referral to Tusla and/or An Garda Síochána.

Role of Childcare Worker

As a childcare worker, you need to be aware that the above signs and symptoms may not occur on a one-off basis and usually there is a pattern of behaviour that alerts you to suspect child abuse. Reasonableness and proper observation play a huge part in such situations. In this respect, the precise recording of observations and the keeping of a reflective diary are essential to the proper care and observation of children in your care.

It is important to note that physical signs may not be evident in cases of sexual abuse due to the nature of the abuse and/or the fact that the disclosure was made some time after the abuse took place.

Where you notice significant changes in a child's behaviour you should be prompted to question why this is so and what you can do to rectify the situation. You should familiarise yourself with the procedures to follow in the facility you are working in and ensure that you follow them correctly where abuse is suspected. Remember also that not every suspicion will be founded and you need to take an objective view of what you see. There may be situations where, for example, a younger child is unable to articulate a worry, and in such circumstances your listening to what the child is actually saying may be a relief to that child and alter the behaviour you thought was out of the ordinary.

Your constant focus must be on the best interests of the child and more specifically the best interests of the child in front of you whose individual needs will change with his or her knowledge, understanding and development, or in the words of the Convention on the Rights of the Child, with his or her 'evolving capacities'.

You also should ensure that you do not unwittingly put yourself in situations where you might be open to an accusation of abuse. In this regard, you should follow the policies and procedures that are set out for your workplace at all times – they are there to protect everybody.

The significance of protecting yourself should also be borne in mind in relation to the passing into law of the National Vetting Bureau (Children and Vulnerable Persons) Act 2012 which applies to anybody who works in childcare or with vulnerable persons. The vetting procedure in the interests of protection of children and vulnerable persons allows for the exchange of information between the National Vetting Bureau and the Gardaí in relation to what is called 'soft' information about a person. This refers to information that does not amount to criminal conviction but may include suspicions that existed but were held to be unsubstantiated. If nothing else, this should serve as a reminder to people working with children or vulnerable people to carefully follow the policies and procedures of the setting they work in so as not to compromise their future job potential.

CHAPTER 6

REPORTING CHILD ABUSE

Children First Act 2015 and Mandated Persons

The Children First Act 2015 introduced the concept of mandated persons in relation to child protection situations. It uses **classes of people** to infer mandated status on them as follows:

1. Registered medical practitioner within the meaning of section 2 of the Medical Practitioners Act 2007.

2. Registered nurse or registered midwife within the meaning of section 2(1) of the Nurses and Midwives Act 2011.

3. Physiotherapist registered in the register of members of that profession.

4. Speech and language therapist registered in the register of members of that profession.

5. Occupational therapist registered in the register of members of that profession.

6. Registered dentist within the meaning of section 2 of the Dentists Act 1985.

7. Psychologist who practises as such and who is eligible for registration in the register (if any) of members of that profession.

8. Social care worker who practises as such and who is eligible for registration in accordance with Part 4 of the Health and Social Care Professionals Act 2005 in the register of that profession.

9. Social worker who practises as such and who is eligible for registration in accordance with Part 4 of the Health and Social Care Professionals Act 2005 in the register (if any) of that profession.

10. Emergency medical technician, paramedic and advanced paramedic registered with the Pre-Hospital Emergency Care Council under the Pre-Hospital Emergency Care Council (Establishment) Order 2000 (S.I. No. 109 of 2000).

11. Probation officer within the meaning of section 1 of the Criminal Justice (Community Service) Act 1983.

12. Teacher registered with the Teaching Council.

13. Member of An Garda Síochána.

14. Guardian *ad litem* appointed in accordance with section 26 of the Child Care Act 1991.

15.   Person employed in any of the following capacities:

(a)   manager of domestic violence shelter;

(b)   manager of homeless provision or emergency accommodation facility;

(c)   manager of asylum seeker accommodation (direct provision) centre;

(d)   addiction counsellor employed by a body funded, wholly or partly, out of moneys provided by the Oireachtas;

(e)   psychotherapist or a person providing counselling who is registered with one of the voluntary professional bodies;

(f)   manager of a language school or other recreational school where children reside away from home;

(g)   member of the clergy (howsoever described) or pastoral care worker (howsoever described) of a church or other religious community;

(h)   director of any institution where a child is detained by an order of a court;

(i)   safeguarding officer, child protection officer or other person (howsoever described) who is employed for the purpose of performing the child welfare and protection function of religious, sporting, recreational, cultural, educational and other bodies and organisations offering services to children;

(j)   child care staff member employed in a pre-school service within the meaning of Part VIIA of the Child Care Act 1991;

(k)   person responsible for the care or management of a youth work service within the meaning of section 2 of the Youth Work Act 2001.

16.   Youth worker who—

(a)   holds a professional qualification that is recognised by the National Qualifications Authority in youth work within the meaning of section 3 of the Youth Work Act 2001 or a related discipline, and

(b)   is employed in a youth work service within the meaning of section 2 of the Youth Work Act 2001.

17.   Foster carer registered with the Agency.

18.   A person carrying on a pre-school service within the meaning of Part VIIA of the Child Care Act 1991.

Any person who falls into any of these categories is a mandated person and has a legal responsibility to make a report of suspected child or vulnerable person abuse. Specifically, the mandated person is required to (a) report the harm of children above a defined threshold (effectively meaning that it does constitute abuse) to Tusla, and (b) assist Tusla, if requested, in assessing a concern that has been the subject of a mandated report.

Services under the Children First Act 2015 that therefore need to put in place robust policies and procedures for people working in them are:

- Early years services
- Schools and centres of education
- Hospitals, hospices and health centres, and other centres providing physical or mental health services to children
- Residential care settings, including residential centres providing care to children with disabilities
- Special care units
- Children detention schools
- Reception or accommodation centres where children seeking asylum may be accommodated
- Domestic violence shelters where children may be accommodated
- Any work or activity which consists of inspecting services provided to a child
- Any inspection, examination or investigation undertaken by the Ombudsman for Children

- Any work or activity which involves providing treatment, therapy or counselling to a child
- Any work or activity which involves providing:
  - Educational, research, training, cultural, recreational, leisure, social or physical activities to children
  - Care or supervision of children
  - Formal consultation with, or formal participation by, a child in matters which affect his or her life
- Any work or activity which involves providing advice or guidance services to a child
- Any work or activity as a minister, priest or other person involved in the advancement of any religious belief
- Any work or activity as a driver, assistant to a driver, conductor or supervisor of children on a vehicle where children travel unaccompanied by a parent or guardian
- Any work or activity as a member of An Garda Síochána whose work involves access to, or contact with, children.

To qualify as a relevant service under the Children First Act 2015, the service provider must employ at least one person to provide that service. This effectively excludes those who work alone without employees as well as activities undertaken in the course of a family or personal relationship for no commercial benefit, e.g. a grandparent who minds their grandchild.

Therefore, you are a mandated person either because the qualification or responsibility you hold classifies you as a mandated person under the 2015 act, or else the place in which you work has specific mandated person status for everybody who works there. It is safe to say that if you are working in a situation where children will be involved, then that work will make you a mandated person and will therefore legally require you to make a disclosure where you suspect child abuse.

Standard Child Abuse Reporting Procedure

Members of the public (who are **not mandated** reporting persons) who suspect child abuse should make a report to Tusla in person, by phone or in writing. Duty social workers are available each day to meet with or talk on the telephone to persons wishing to report child protection concerns. In the event of an emergency or the non-availability of Tusla staff, a report may be made to An Garda Síochána at any garda station.

Section 14 of the Children First Act 2015 directs a **mandated person** to report a mandated concern to Tusla 'as soon as practicable' after becoming aware of the potential of harm to a child or vulnerable person. Tusla requires a specific report form to be filled out, and the information supplied by you, if you are a mandated reporting person, should include as much relevant information about the child so that Tusla does not need to go back to you for more information and can instead start its investigation immediately and independently.

The 'Tusla Child Protection and Welfare Report' (see Appendix 3) is used for staff or volunteers in organisations that work with children or are in contact with children. It is a requirement for every person who works with children to receive child protection training and regular updates on changes to Children First Guidance 2017 or subsequent versions. The guiding principles regarding reporting child abuse or neglect may be summarised as follows:

(i) the safety and well-being of the child must take priority;

(ii) reports must be made without delay to Tusla Child and Family Services.

If you are reporting suspected abuse, you should provide as much as possible of the following information as required on the Tusla Child Protection and Welfare Report so that Tusla can start enquiries if need be:

- Names and addresses of the child, parents/ carers and any other children in the family

- Name and address of the person alleged to be causing harm to the child

- A full account of the current concern about the child's safety or welfare

- The source of any information that is being discussed with Tusla

- Dates of any incidents being reported
- Circumstances in which the incident or concern arose
- Any explanation offered to account for the risk, injury or concern
- The child's own statement, if relevant (this would be in the case where a child made a disclosure, in which case you do not question a child but only record what they say)
- Any other information about the family, particularly any difficulties that the family may be experiencing that you may be aware of (remember that those difficulties may have nothing to do with what is happening and staff should always be professional in their dealings)
- Any factors relating to the family that could be considered supportive or protective (e.g. helpful family members, neighbours or services)
- Name of the child's school
- Name of the child's general practitioner
- Your involvement with the child and parents/carers
- Details of any action already taken in relation to the child's safety and welfare
- Names and addresses of any agencies or key person that you may already know are involved with the family
- Your name, address, telephone number, occupation and relationship with the family.

Co-operation with Parents/Carers

A mandated person is **not** required under the Children First Act 2015 to inform the family that a report under the legislation is being submitted to Tusla or An Garda Síochána, even though it is considered good practice to tell the family the report is being submitted and the reasons why. The act also does not require you to inform the family if doing so is likely to endanger the child and put them at further risk. In making your decision on whether to inform the family, it should be remembered that co-operation with the family is essential in order to ensure the safety of the child and this is more likely to be achieved if professionals can develop an open and honest relationship with parents/carers.

In cases of emergency, where a child appears to be at immediate and serious risk, and a duty social worker is unavailable, An Garda Síochána should be contacted. Under no circumstances should a child be left in a dangerous situation pending Tusla intervention.

Involvement in a child protection assessment can be difficult for parents/carers. Families may have the right to know what is said about them and to contribute to important decisions about their lives and those of their children. Sensitivity must be used, and parents/carers should be made fully aware of what is expected of them. Therefore it is a requirement that all matters of this nature are approached with professionalism.

The Consequences of Not Making a Report

Any reasonable concern or suspicion of abuse or neglect must be dealt with. Ignoring the signals or failing to intervene may result in ongoing harm to a child and can under Section 176 of the Criminal Justice Act 2006 lead to a criminal conviction for a person who recklessly endangers a child, where that person is deemed guilty of:

(a)   causing or permitting any child to be placed or left in a situation which creates a substantial risk to the child of being a victim of serious harm or sexual abuse, or

(b)   failing to take reasonable steps to protect a child from such a risk while knowing that the child is in such a situation.

The penalty under the Criminal Justice Act 2006 includes a fine and/or imprisonment of up to ten years.

This is further reinforced by Section 2 of the Criminal Justice (Withholding of Information on Offences Against Children and Vulnerable Adults) Act 2012, which makes it a criminal offence if:

(a)   he or she knows or believes that an offence, that is a Schedule 1 offence, has been committed by another person against a child, and

(b)   he or she has information which he or she knows or believes might be of material assistance in securing the apprehension, prosecution or conviction of that other person for that offence

and fails without reasonable excuse to disclose that information as soon as it is practicable to do so to a member of the Garda Síochána.

In this outline, a Schedule 1 offence is defined in the act as 'an offence that is an arrestable offence', and the act provides a list of such offences which include most of the offences covered under the child abuse definitions above and more.

It is never sufficient to do nothing when you suspect that a child is or has been the subject of an abuse, as the consequences for that individual child may stay with them for the rest of their lives, and certainly has the potential to interfere with that child reaching their best potential. Doing nothing does not serve the child's best interests, as Irish legislation outlines.

The Children First Guidance 2017 outlines that:

both public and private organisations that are providing services to children should consider appointing a designated liaison person in keeping with best practice in child safeguarding. This person will be the resource person for any staff member or volunteer who has child protection concerns and will liaise with outside agencies. The designated liaison person should be knowledgeable about child protection and should be provided with any training considered necessary to fulfil this role.

Organisations who have employees who are mandated persons under the Children First Act 2015 must ensure that training specifically on the statutory responsibilities of mandated persons under the act is made available to them. In the case of organisations that have a nominated designated liaison person or deputy designated liaison person, they should ensure that they receive adequate child protection and welfare information and training to enable them to undertake this role. The designated liaison person is responsible for ensuring that reporting procedures within your organisation are followed, so that child welfare and protection concerns are referred promptly to Tusla. The designated liaison person should record all concerns or allegations of child abuse brought to their attention as well as the actions taken in relation to a concern or allegation of child abuse, and if, as the designated liaison person, they decide not to report a concern to Tusla, the following steps should be taken:

- The reasons for not reporting should be recorded
- Any actions taken as a result of the concern should be recorded
- The employee or volunteer who raised the concern should be given a clear written explanation of the reasons why the concern is not being reported to Tusla

- The employee or volunteer should be advised that if they remain concerned about the situation, they are free to make a report to Tusla or An Garda Síochána.

Being a Designated Person and a Mandated Person

The Children First 2017 Guidance document outlines that some designated liaison persons will be working in organisations where mandated persons are also employed, in which case the statutory obligation of mandated persons to report under the Children First Act 2015 has to be discharged by the **mandated person** and cannot be discharged by the designated liaison person on their behalf.

Mandated persons may also have the role of designated liaison persons in some organisation, and in those situations they must fulfil the statutory obligations of a mandated person. This means that if, as a designated liaison person, you are made aware of a concern about a child that meets or exceeds the thresholds of harm for mandated reporting, you have a statutory obligation to make a report to Tusla arising from your position as a mandated person. This is akin to having a dual responsibility.

Additionally, mandated persons have statutory obligations to report mandated concerns, and they can make a report jointly with another person, whether that other person is a mandated person or not. In effect, this means that *a mandated person can make a joint report with a designated liaison person.*

The process sounds complicated, but it can be made very simple if the organisation draws up robust policies and procedures in relation to child safeguarding as outlined in the guidance document. Staff should be aware of those policies and procedures, which should be updated and reviewed regularly, and staff should also be trained and have that training updated regularly. Every opportunity should be taken to ensure that the organisation is acting in the best interests of the children within its care.

Those involved in childcare should always remember that the children in your care depend on you, and that when you chose your profession you undertook to follow the standards and ethics of that profession. This includes a duty of care to support and protect the children in your charge and to put their interests and welfare about all other considerations.

CHAPTER 7

CHILDREN ACT 2001

Where the Child Care Act 1991 and the Children Act 2001 are referred to together, they can be called the Child Care Acts 1991 and 2001.

The 2001 act was updated in November 2017. The reason it was updated was because the responsibility for children had been under the HSE. That meant the Minister for Health was in charge of all things to do with children yet everything to do with children was not all about their health. From 2011 this was changed so that the Minister responsible for children would take over all things to do with children. Tusla was set up under the Child and Family Agency Act 2013 to make this change legally effective.

The act provides for additional procedures in relation to children, including:

- Regulation in relation to private foster care homes
- Inspections of private foster homes
- A system of diversion programmes, to be administered by An Garda Síochána, where a child between the age of criminal responsibility and eighteen accepts responsibility for a criminal wrongdoing and consents to the appointment of a juvenile liaison officer

- Issuing of formal and informal cautions to children
- Setting out the duties of An Garda Síochána in relation to underage children in custody
- The separation of children from adults while in custody
- Setting out the procedures and duties of the Children Court
- Use of parental supervision orders on parents where there is 'wilful failure of the child's parents to take care of or control the child'
- Use of day care orders, intensive care orders, detention centre and detention schools where appropriate.

Family Welfare Conferences

The Children Act 2001 allows under Section 9 for family conferences to facilitate the process of child protection or special care and attention which they might not receive unless an order is made in respect of them. The act sets out the procedures to be applied and allows that the following persons concerned with the child's welfare shall be entitled to attend:

Section 9(1)

(a)   the child in respect of whom the conference is being convened,

(b)   the parents or guardian of the child,

(c)   any guardian *ad litem* appointed for the child,

(d)   such other relative of the child as may be determined by the coordinator, after consultation with the child and the child's parents or guardian,

(e)   an employee or employees of the Child and Family Agency,

(f)   any other person who, in the opinion of the coordinator, after consultation with the child and his or her parents or guardian, would make a positive contribution to the conference because of the person's knowledge of the child or the child's family or because of his or her particular expertise.

Section 9(2)

If, before or during a family welfare conference, the coordinator is of the opinion that the presence or continued presence of any person is not in the best interests of the conference or the child, the coordinator may exclude that person from participation or further participation in the conference.

Once again we see that the best interests of the child are to the forefront. As well as that, giving children the opportunity to be present, to have representation and to voice their opinions when matters relating to them are being discussed is in line with Article 12 of the Convention on the Rights of the Child.

In defining the functions of a family welfare conference, the act states in Section 8(1) that it will seek:

> . . . to bring together the child in respect of whom the conference is being held, his or her parents or guardian, such other family members, relatives and other persons as appropriate and the facilitator with a view to—
>
> (i)   establishing why the child became involved in the behaviour that gave rise to his or her admission to the Programme,
>
> (ii) discussing how the parents or guardian, family members, relatives or any other person could help to prevent the child from becoming involved in further such behaviour, and
>
> (iii) where appropriate, reviewing the child's behaviour since his or her admission to the Programme . . .

What is paramount in these situations is that the effort made by authorities gets the child into the best possible care situation in relation to that child's circumstances. The result of such conferences may be a special care order or a temporary or interim care order, which is allowed for in the act.

Parental Supervision Orders

Under the 2001 act, a parental supervision order may require the parents of the child to do any or all of the following:

(a)   to undergo treatment for alcohol or other substance abuse, where facilities for such treatment are reasonably available,

(b)   to participate in any course that is reasonably available for the improvement of parenting skills,

(c)   adequately and properly to control or supervise the child to the best of their ability, except where the terms of any community sanction imposed on the child make such control or supervision impracticable,

(d)   to comply with any other instructions of the court that would in its opinion assist in preventing the child from committing further offences.

A parental supervision order will be made for a period not exceeding six months. During this period, the parents will be supported in their efforts to learn or correct behaviour or situations that may have resulted in the child's behaviour – the reason for this process (always bearing in mind that the Constitution states that the child's place is in the family). It is also the case that the child now has rights under Article 42A that must be taken into account. The idea is that education to a higher level of child supervision by parents is probably fair in situations where those parents may have been the victims of child neglect or abuse themselves, and thus may not ever have had the opportunity to observe and learn the skills of good parenting. Just as easily, those parents may not be in a position psychologically to deal with issues that can arise, and so this case support and supervision can help to re-establish familial supports for the child, which would be in the child's best interests.

Supervision orders allow for some overview of the progress that is being made by all concerned and this support for the process of rehabilitation is very much in the child's best interests. It is clear to see that the essence of the Irish Constitution and the ideals set out in the UN Convention on the Rights of the Child have been taken seriously in these provisions.

CHAPTER 8

CHILD CARE REGULATIONS

Some issues are dealt with by regulation rather than by the enactment of a law. Changes to a law must be passed by both Houses of the Oireachtas and then signed and agreed to by the President, as outlined in the Constitution. This is often a lengthy process and open debate on small changes to operating conditions may result in further changes that restrict the potential effectiveness of the proposed amendment. The quicker way to change such detail is to put them in regulations, which are still binding but are more flexible in development.

Child Care Regulations provide for standards of service, upkeep and care for any setting defined as pre-school. The regulations define a pre-school child to be one under the age of six who is not in full-time education. Any person working with preschool children must follow these regulations and they form part of the care contract for each child.

It is not possible within the confines of this book to carry out a full analysis of every regulation contained in Child Care Regulations as they are detailed and involve many conditions for children being cared for by people other than their parents; however, all regulations should be read in context to get a full understanding of the care and safety requirements that must be adhered to when running a childcare service. Tusla regularly updates regulation, and keeping up to date with changes is the responsibility of the pre-school operator and the people working within the setting.

To date, the following regulations have contributed to the systems that operate in any pre-school in Ireland:

- Child Care Regulations 2006
- Child Care (Pre-School Services) (No.2) Regulations 2006
- Child Care Act 1991 (Early Years Services) Regulations 2016
- Child Care Act 1991 (Early Years Services) (Amendment) Regulations 2016
- Child Care Act 1991 (Early Years Services) (Registration of School Age Services) Regulations 2018

The regulations are there to protect children and to ensure the safety and welfare of each child. Inspections are carried out regularly to ensure that the required standards are maintained.

The remainder of this chapter focuses on some of the more significant details to be found in regulations.

Carer/Child Ratios

The regulations changed the carer/child ratios that exist for different settings. The new ratios that came into effect are set out in the table below.

Age Range	Carer/Child Ratio
Full or part-time day care service	
Full-time = > 5+ hours per day	
Part-time = > 2½–5 hours per day	
0–1 year	1:3
1–2 years	1:5
2–3 years	1:6
3–6 years	1:8
Sessional pre-school service	
Sessional = > up to 3½ hours per day	
0–1 year	1:3
1–2½ years	1:5
2½–6 years	1:11 (changed to 11 for ECCE)
Pre-school service in a drop-in centre or in a temporary drop-in centre*	
0–6 years	1:4
Childminding service	
0–6 years	1:5 maximum, which would include own child, with conditions regarding the range of ages
Overnight pre-school service	
0–1 year	1:3
1–6 years	1:5

*Maximum group size is twenty-four and other detailed conditions apply

This table does not reveal the full story in relation to the carer/child ratios as the regulations allow Tusla to set a maximum number that can be cared for in a particular service – often this may happen because of space requirements.

Minimum Space Requirements

The regulations also specify a minimum space per child. The space requirements relate to clear floor space per child. Clear floor space means the area available for children's work, play and movement and does not include furniture that is surplus to the requirements of the child or permanent fixtures. Places such as kitchens, toilets and sleeping or utility areas are not included in the space calculation in relation to a child.

Age Range of Child	Clear Floor Space Required
0–1 year	3.5 square metres
1–2 years	2.8 square metres
2–3 years	2.35 square metres
3–6 years	2.3 square metres

Additionally, all new services who register their intention to run a pre-school service after 30 June 2016 must provide a suitable, safe and secure outdoor area that children can access every day. If that outdoor space is not available in the actual pre-school service, then there must be an alternative outdoor space provided that is accessible daily.

Care of Children

The regulations set out specific requirements in relation to the care of children in pre-school facilities in order to protect the welfare of such children. These requirements include:

- A suitably equipped first aid box for children must be kept on the premises
- There must be suitably qualified staff (minimum QQI Level 5 qualification) as well as suitably qualified persons must be employed
- Appropriate vetting of staff, students and volunteers who have access to children must be undertaken before they have access to a child in a pre-school service. In the case of a staff member, this should refer to past employers; in relation to students and volunteers, it should be by reference to reputable sources. Whether employee, contractor or student, National Vetting Bureau procedures must have been followed and two suitable references must be verified and held on file for inspection purposes.
- No corporal punishment is allowed
- No disrespectful, degrading, exploitive, intimidating, emotionally or physically harmful or neglectful practices are to be carried out in respect of any child
- Written policies and procedures (which must be reviewed at intervals of not more than one year and must be kept on file for three years after a

review takes place) must be in place in relation to challenging behaviour and other specified headings such as:

- Infection control
- Safe sleep
- Fire safety
- Inclusion
- Outings if they are undertaken
- Accidents and incidents
- Authorisation to collect children
- Staff absences
- Internet, photographic and recording devices use
- Recruitment
- Risk management
- Settling in
- Staff training
- Supervision
- Complaints procedures

- Tusla may set the maximum number of children that may be cared for in the space provided
- Proper insurance must be in place in each setting
- A register of children must be kept, recording the following details in respect of each child:
  - Name and date of birth
  - Date first attended the service
  - Date ceased to attend the service

- Name and address and operation time (the time the pre-school is open) telephone number of parent or guardian or relative or friend of the child
- Authorisation for collection
- Details of illness, disability, allergy or special need
- Name and telephone number of child's registered general practitioner (doctor)
- Record of immunisation, if any, received by the child
- Written consent for appropriate medical treatment in emergencies

• Suitable heating, ventilation, light, sanitary accommodation, drainage, sewage disposal, waste disposal and storage must be provided in each pre-school facility

• Furniture must be adequate and work and play equipment must be of non-toxic materials, in a proper state of repair and in a clean and hygienic condition.

School Age Services

The Child Care Act 1991 (Early Years Services) (Registration of School Age Services) Regulations 2018 came into force on 18 February 2019 and means that anyone who caters for school-age children (even if only for one hour per day) must now be registered with Tusla, the Child and Family Agency.

The aim of these regulations is to allow proper procedures to be applied in after-school services that are being provided or planned.

Minimum adult–child ratios are outlined as 1:12 but this depends on how may pre-school children are included in the service. The limit is altered in the case of pre-school children being included as follows:

No. pre-school children being cared for	Maximum no. of school-age children
0	12
1	10
2	7
3	5
4	2
5	1

School age regulations apply to children from ages 4–15.

Childminders do not have to register with Tusla if they care for a mix within their maximum of six children as follows:

No. pre-school children cared for	Maximum no. of school-age children
1	5
2	4
3*	3

Maximum two babies under fifteen months

New 2018 School Age Provision Requirements:

- There is no minimum space size specified yet but rooms should not be overcrowded
- Policies on complaints, administration of medicines, infection control, managing behaviour, dropping off and collecting children, purpose and function and fire safety must be in place
- Access to outdoor space must be provided
- Insurance must be in place
- References for all staff must be in place including from last employer
- New ratios apply to these services

These 2018 regulations are an evolving piece of work and changes can be expected after consultation with providers, but they are a step towards ensuring that the welfare and safety of children in such services are of a high standard and facilitate the best interests of every child attending such services.

CHAPTER 9

MENTAL HEALTH ACTS 2001 AND 2018

The Mental Health Acts 2001 and 2018 refer to the original Mental Health Act 2001, which provided for the involuntary admission of patients suffering from mental disorders to approved centres of care. It also provides for review of such people and the establishment of a Mental Health Commission. The Mental Health (Amendment) Act 2018 alters some provisions of the original 2001 act specifically in relation to the treatment of children.

The act defines a mental disorder as follows:

3.   (1) In this Act 'mental disorder' means mental illness, severe dementia or significant intellectual disability where—

(a)   because of the illness, disability or dementia, there is a serious likelihood of the person concerned causing immediate and serious harm to himself or herself or to other persons, or

(b)   (i) because of the severity of the illness, disability or dementia, the judgement of the person concerned is so impaired that failure to admit the person to an approved centre would be likely to lead to a serious deterioration in his or her condition or would prevent the administration of appropriate treatment that could be given only by such admission, and

(ii) the reception, detention and treatment of the person concerned in an approved centre would be likely to benefit or alleviate the condition of that person to a material extent.

(2) In *subsection (1)*—

'mental illness' means a state of mind of a person which affects the person's thinking, perceiving, emotion or judgement and which seriously impairs the mental function of the person to the extent that he or she requires care or medical treatment in his or her own interest or in the interest of other persons;

'severe dementia' means a deterioration of the brain of a person which significantly impairs the intellectual function of the person thereby affecting thought, comprehension and memory and which includes severe psychiatric or behavioural symptoms such as physical aggression;

> 'significant intellectual disability' means a state of arrested or incomplete development of mind of a person which includes significant impairment of intelligence and social functioning and abnormally aggressive or seriously irresponsible conduct on the part of the person.

The 2018 act, which was necessary to take account of the Assisted Decision-Making (Capacity) Act 2015, altered the original Mental Health Act 2001 by ensuring that the capacity of the person involved is not presumed away but rather that they are enabled to make the best decision on the basis of their rights, existing capacity, welfare and best interests even if they need assistance to make those decisions.

While it pre-dates the Disability Act 2005, which gives a more concise definition of disability, it was never envisaged that the Mental Health Act 2001 would be used to detain people with an intellectual disability which is not 'significant', as defined above. It is always important when reading any act to check the definition section at the beginning of the act to ascertain who it applies to and any technical definitions such as above.

Involuntary Admission of Children

Section 23 of the Mental Health Act 2001 states that where the parents of a child or one of the parents or a person acting *in loco parentis* wish to take a child who is a voluntary patient out of an

approved centre, and a registered medical practitioner, registered nurse on the centre's staff or a
consultant psychiatrist is of the opinion that the
child is suffering from a mental disorder as defined
above, then the child may be kept and placed in
the custody of the Health Service Executive (HSE).

It goes on to state that where this happens and
the HSE wishes to detain the child under Section
25 of the act (dealing with involuntary admission
to approved centres), then the HSE must apply to
the District Court for the area within three days of
the child being taken into the HSE's care for such
an involuntary detention order.

The granting in court of such an involuntary detention order under the Mental Health Act 2001 reflects
the ideals of the Convention on the Rights of the
Child. Under Section 25 of the act, the court
requires specific details of the mental disorder
claimed and, if satisfied that, as the act states,

(a)   the child is suffering from a mental
        disorder, and

(b)   the child requires treatment which he or
        she is unlikely to receive unless an order is
        made under this section,

then the HSE can apply to the District Court for an
order of detention of the child in an approved
centre, and should only do so if a competent
consultant psychiatrist (who is not a relation of the
child) has examined the child and submitted a
report. However, the act also provides that if the

parent(s) or somebody *in loco parentis* refuses to consent to the examination by the consultant psychiatrist – or where no such person (parent or person acting *in loco parentis)* can be found, the HSE can apply without the prior examination of a consultant psychiatrist – and the court can then direct that the examination takes place and that the report be brought to court within a specific period of time.

Where the court does receive this report within the time limit set, it will make an order for the child's detention for a period of not more than twenty-one days. Where such order has been made and the HSE wishes to extend it before it expires, the court may extend the period for three months and after that for a period not over six months, which may then be extended for further periods of six months if the court is satisfied that the child has been examined by a consultant psychiatrist who is not a relation of the child and that report is given to the court, and the court, having read the report, is satisfied the child is still suffering from a mental disorder.

Throughout this process, psychosurgery and electroconvulsive therapy cannot be used on the child without the approval of the courts.

The Mental Health Act 2001 states that in all such proceedings Section 24 of the Child Care Act 1991 shall apply, which states that 'having regard to the rights and duties of parents, whether under the Constitution or otherwise', the court will:

(a)   regard the welfare of the child as the first and paramount consideration, and

(b)   in so far as is practicable, give due consideration, having regard to his age and understanding, to the wishes of the child.

The Mental Health (Amendment) Act 2018 specifically states with the insertion of a new section 4A that the guiding principles in respect of children are as follows:

(1) In making a decision under this Act concerning the care or treatment of a child (including the making of a specific application under section 25(1) and a decision of the Court to make an order under section 25(6) authorising the detention of a child in an approved centre), the best interests of the child shall be the paramount consideration.

(2) Notwithstanding the generality of subsection (1), in making a decision under this Act concerning the care or treatment of a child (including the making of a specific application under section 25(1) and a decision of the Court to make an order under section 25(6) authorising the detention of a child in an approved centre), due regard shall also be given to the following principles (in this Act referred to as 'guiding principles'), namely the need—

1.   (a) for every child to have access to health services that have as the aim

of those services, the delivery of the highest attainable standard of child mental health,

(b) in the case of a child who is capable of forming his or her own views, to consult, where practicable, the child at each stage of diagnosis and treatment and give due weight to—

    (i) his or her views, and

    (ii) his or her will or preferences,

having regard to the age and maturity of that child,

(c) in so far as is practicable, to provide care and treatment—

    (i) in an age-appropriate environment, and

    (ii) in close proximity to the child's home or family, as appropriate,

(d) for the child to receive the least intrusive treatment possible in the least restrictive environment practicable, and

(e) to respect the right of the child to dignity, bodily integrity, privacy and autonomy.

This process is in line with the Convention on the Rights of the Child in that there is periodic review of the detention of the child and the best interests of the child will be taken into consideration.

There are two further issues in relation to children detained at approved centres under the Mental Health Act 2001.

Medicine

Medicine administered to a child in involuntary detention at an approved centre to relieve the mental disorder can only be given for a continuous period of three months unless the continuation of the medicine is either approved by the consultant psychiatrist responsible for the care of the child or approved (in a specific form determined by the Mental Health Commission) by another consultant psychiatrist after the matter has been referred to them by the consultant psychiatrist responsible for the care of the child. The procedure must be followed every three months so that authorisation and approval is obtained continuously.

Bodily Restraint and Seclusion

The Mental Health Commission makes rules regarding the use of mechanical means of restraint (such as seat belts) and seclusion of a patient. Such rules must be followed where it is deemed necessary 'for the purposes of treatment or to prevent the patient from injuring himself or herself or others'.

Throughout the Mental Health Act 2001 and the Mental Health (Amendment) Act 2018, the focus on the best interests of the child is evident, and while this is an emotive topic to deal with in relation to any child, the rules fulfil the ideals in the UN Convention on the Rights of the Child because of this principle and also because each detention is reviewed periodically, as is the administration of medicine.

CHAPTER 10

GUARDIANSHIP OF INFANTS ACTS 1964 TO 1997

The concept of children within adult relationships and family situations in Ireland has changed considerably over the last number of decades. The Guardianship of Infants Act 1964, although pre-dating the Child Care Act 1991, affects some of the actions that can be taken in relation to children: the right of access, custody and guardianship, particularly in relation to children who are born when their parents are not married. Indeed, the contents of the 1964 act are sometimes unknown to the fathers of children until a problem arises. This act, however, was very dated and to a certain extent was more reflective of the Ireland of old, where being an unmarried parent was deemed to be unacceptable.

The 1964 act has been revised, which is why it can now be referred to as the Guardianship of Infants Act 1964 to 1997. That does not mean that changes have not been made to bring the act up to date to reflect changes made by other more recent acts such as the Civil Partnership and Certain Right and Obligations of Cohabitants Act 2010, the Adoption Act 2010 and the Children and Family Relationships Act 2015. Those changes now mean that application of the act is more reflective of different family structures in today's Ireland and also of a more global Ireland where children's parents may live in other countries, or be involved in other relationships or other families.

Distinct concepts that arise include:

- Access, which means actually having interactions with the child and is now a right of the child. Access would be very relevant to grandparents, for instance, who can apply to the courts to have this granted.
- Custody, which means the normal day-to-day care and control of the child.
- Guardianship, which means the right to make decisions about how the child is brought up. It relates in particular to the ability, duty and right to decide issues such as the child's upbringing, religion, schooling, etc.

One of the most important aspects of this act is its provision that the mother of a child born out of marriage is the automatic guardian of that child. The same automatic right does not apply to the father of that child. Rather, the natural father must apply to the courts to be made a guardian of the child, which could be done jointly with the mother but only with the consent and co-operation of that mother. In the case of cohabiting couples, there may have been an adoption order and in that case, the rights do exist.

A father seeking to be made a guardian of his child must convince the court that he is prepared to protect the welfare of the child – this means the 'child's religious, moral, intellectual, physical and social welfare' (in other words, it is not just about making maintenance payments).

Where a guardian is appointed by will or deed (such as when the mother dies and appoints the natural father as guardian, also known as testamentary guardianship) and afterwards that person is deemed not to have the child's welfare as the first and paramount consideration, then the courts can appoint a new guardian.

The act allows the child to be consulted in relation to guardianship issues where appropriate and in line with their age and level of understanding of the issues involved.

Under the act, there is also a distinction between access and guardianship. A father can have access (the right to spend time with the child) and still not be the child's guardian. This could be relevant in legal issues that might arise in childcare.

A person working with children in any setting must understand that under the Guardianship of Infants Act 1964 to 1997, a father may have lots of input into a child's care arrangements – such as seeing, delivering and collecting the child – but he might not be the child's guardian and cannot make decisions on the welfare of that child. It is important for legal reasons to understand this distinction. That is also why it is essential that the records in relation to a child in a setting are up to date and take account of such issues, which can be ascertained by suitable questions on an application form, provided that there is no implication in relation to the application as a result of the questions. The facts just need to be ascertained to ensure the best interests of the child are being met, and to ensure that the setting allows for access to both parents, a right of the child under the UN Convention on the Rights of the Child.

CHAPTER 11

STATUS OF CHILDREN ACT 1987

The Status of Children Act 1987, which amended the Family Law (Maintenance of Spouses and Children) Act 1976, sought to define what exactly a family is in Irish legislation. Section 46 states:

(1)   Where a woman gives birth to a child –

   (a)   during a subsisting marriage to which she is a party, or

   (b)   within the period of ten months after the termination, by death or otherwise, of a marriage to which she is a party,

   then the husband of the marriage shall be presumed to be the father of the child unless the contrary is proved on the balance of probabilities.

In other words, in a married couple relationship it is usually presumed that the husband is the father of his wife's children unless otherwise proven.

(2)   Notwithstanding *subsection (1)* of this section, where a married woman, being a woman who is living apart from her husband under –

(a)   a decree of divorce *a mensa et thoro*, or

(b)   a deed of separation,

gives birth to a child ***more than ten months*** after the decree was granted or the deed was executed as the case may be, then her husband shall be ***deemed not to be the father*** of the child unless the contrary is proved otherwise on the balance of probabilities.

In effect, this means that where a couple separate by divorce or mutual separation, having been married, and a child is born more than ten months after the separation or divorce, then the ex-husband is presumed not to be the father of the child unless otherwise proven (and therefore conversely if the child is born *within ten months* of such separation or divorce, then the ex-husband *is presumed* to be the father of the child unless otherwise proven).

(3)   Notwithstanding *subsection (1)* of this section, where –

(a)   the birth of a child is registered in a register maintained under the Births and Deaths Registration Acts, 1863 to 1987, and

(b)   the name of the person is entered as the father of the child on the register so maintained, then the person whose name is entered shall be presumed to be the father of the child unless the contrary is proved on the balance of probabilities.

In other words, if the father is recorded as such on a legally correct register, then he is presumed to be the father unless otherwise proven.

Section 49 states:

(1) In the case of a child whose parents were not married to each other at the date of his birth or at any time during the period of ten months before his birth, no person shall as father of the child be required to give information concerning the birth.

(2) The registrar shall not enter in the register the name of a person as father of a child to whom subsection (1) of this section relates except –

   (a) at the joint request of the mother and the person acknowledging himself to be the father of the child, or

   (b) at the request of the mother on production of –

      (i) a declaration in the prescribed form made by the mother stating that that person is the father of the child, and

        (ii) a statutory declaration made by that person acknowledging himself to be the father of the child,

or

(c)   at the request of that person on production of –

        (i) a declaration in the prescribed form by that person acknowledging himself to be the father of the child, and

        (ii) a statutory declaration made by the mother stating that that person is the father of the child,

or

(d)   at the request of the mother or that person, which shall in either case be made in writing, on production of a certified copy of any court order in respect of proceedings to which section 45 of the Status of Children Act 1987, relates, naming that person as the father of the child.

This process is further complicated by the possibilities posed by adoption where a declaration can now be acquired stating that the adoptive parents are the parents of the child. This can have implications in relation to inheritances and other administrative processes in law and may well be sought by the adoptive parents to ensure that complications do not arise after their death, for instance.

In line with more modern parentage issues, there is also provision that DNA (deoxyribonucleic acid) taken by

(a)　a swab from the mouth

(b)　a sample of saliva or hair (other than pubic hair) or

(c)　a blood sample

can now also allow a declaration to be made by the courts of parentage of a child where the matter is in dispute.

Further complications in relation to this concept of parentage may arise where the child is born in a donor-conceived process of Donor Assisted Human Reproduction (DAHR) but this complicated issue need not necessarily affect your work with individual children in your setting. While the matter of parentage can have implications for the parents in such situations, it does not alter the necessity of your own concentration on the best interests of the child with whom you work, whoever the parent may be. Your information will be contained in the records of that child and may well reflect the processes described in law as above, but will not alter your professional responsibilities to ensure that the child is safe, well cared for, assisted in the development of their evolving capacities and given a say in issues that relate to them. Your interaction may never be informed by any of the complicated issues already mentioned, which may never be brought to your attention, and in which case do not involve your care contract.

In essence, other than in the last two examples of adoption and DAHR, in most cases in Ireland the father does not have to declare himself as the father if he does not want to, and he cannot be forced to do so unless proper procedures are followed in law. In relation to a child in a childcare setting, childcare workers should always ensure that they are informed about the policies and procedures of the setting in this regard and follow them to the best of their abilities.

CHAPTER 12

ADOPTION ACTS

The concept of the 'welfare of the child' is also a factor in the Adoption Act 1988, which provides that in exceptional cases where the parents for physical or moral reasons have failed in their duty to the child, that child can be adopted by people who will take the place of those parents.

Section 3 of the Adoption Act 1988, which is updated by Section 54 of the Adoption Act 2010, states that the High Court can make an order for adoption of a child in extreme circumstances where it is satisfied

(1) that—

    (a) for a continuous period of not less than 36 months immediately preceding the time of the making of the application, the parents of the child to whom the declaration under *section 53 (1)* relates, have failed in their duty towards the child to such an extent that the safety and welfare of the child is likely to be prejudicially affected,

    (b) there is no reasonable prospect that the parents will be able to care for the child in an manner that will not prejudicially affect his or her safety or welfare,

(c)   such failure constitutes an abandonment on the part of the parents of all parental rights, whether under the Constitution or otherwise, with respect to the child,

(d)   by reason of such failure, the State, as guardian of the common good, should supply the place of the parents,

(e)   the child—

    (i)   at the time of the making of the application, is in the custody of and has a home with the applicants, and

    (ii)   for a continuous period of not less than eighteen months immediately preceding that time, has been in the custody of and has had a home with the applicants,

and

(f)   that the adoption of the child by the applicants is an appropriate means by which to supply the place of the parents,

the High Court may, if it so thinks fit and is satisfied, having had due regard for the rights, whether under the Constitution or otherwise, of the persons concerned (including the natural and imprescriptible rights of the child), that it would be in the best interests of the child to do so, make an order authorising the making of an adoption order in relation to the child in favour of the applicants.

(2) Before making an order under *subsection (1)*, the Court shall, in so far as is practicable, give due consideration, having regard to his age and understanding, to the wishes of the child concerned.

It needs to be emphasised that this applies in exceptional circumstances and that such actions are clearly based on the best interests of the child, comply with the constitutional rights of the child and indeed a parent's rights and duties to the child under the Constitution. It should not be assumed that the child is given away to strangers and there must already exist a situation where the child has been in the care of the adoptee parents for at least eighteen months prior to such adoption. This can sometimes apply to the grandparents of the child in question, who may have taken over the care of the child due to their own child's inability or unwillingness to care for the welfare of the child.

As has already been noted in this book, family life in Ireland today can be structured in many different ways, including foreign adoption, civil partners and cohabiting people or couples who may also want to adopt the children with whom they live. (A cohabiting couple refers to two adults who are cohabitants of each other and who have been living together as cohabitants for a continuous period of not less than three years.)

Interestingly, in Section 37 subsection 5 of the act as adjusted by the Adoption (Amendment) Act 2017, we see the definition of a 'step parent'. The section now provides for the following:

(5)   A person may make an application for an adoption order in respect of a child where, at the date of the application—

(a)   the person is—

(i)   a spouse of a parent of the child,

(ii)   a civil partner of a parent of the child, or

(iii)   a cohabitant in a cohabiting couple where the other cohabitant is a parent of the child,

and

(b)   the child, in respect of whom the adoption order is sought, has a home with the child's parent and that person (in this Act referred to as a 'step parent'), for a continuous period of not less than 2 years.

(6) The Authority, having regard to the particular circumstances of the case may accept an application for an adoption order in respect of a child notwithstanding that the child has not a home with the child's parent and that step parent, for a continuous period of not less than 2 years at the date of the application.

CHAPTER 13

DOMESTIC VIOLENCE ACT 2018

This act replaces the previous Domestic Violence Act 1996 and the Domestic Violence (Amendment) Act 2002. The 2018 act moves Ireland closer to ratifying the Council of Europe Convention on preventing and combatting violence against women and domestic violence, known as the Istanbul Convention. This act also introduces a new offence of 'coercive control', which relates to non-violent control in intimate relationships based on an abuse of trust in that intimate relationship. The act also introduces a new criminal offence of 'forced marriage'.

Bearing in mind that a child witness of domestic violence will have suffered abuse by virtue of the fact that they have witnessed domestic violence, it is also necessary that childcare workers should have some grasp of the procedures in cases of domestic violence.

Under the Domestic Violence Act 1996, as extended by the Domestic Violence Act 2018, there are a number of orders that can be obtained in cases of domestic violence.

Safety Orders

A safety order can apply for five years and can be extended before the five years expire for another five years or some shorter time as may be decided. Such an order stops the person carrying out the violent act from doing more or threatening violence against the person being abused, watching or besetting the place the person resides at and following or communicating (including by electronic means) with the person to whom the order is granted. Provided there are reasonable grounds for thinking the person's safety or welfare is at risk, safety orders are available to:

- A husband or wife who is being subjected to violence (remember that both men and women can be the victims of domestic violence), can apply on their own behalf or on behalf of a child
- Either parties of an unmarried couple (i.e. civil partners)
- A person in an intimate relationship with the party against whom the safety order is required prior to the application for the safety order
- A parent against an adult child
- A person who has a non-contractual relationship and lives with the other person (a lodger or tenant)
- Relatives who live together, against each other
- Tusla, on somebody's behalf.

Barring Orders

A barring order requires the violent person to leave and not re-enter the family home, not use threatening behaviour, not molest and not be in the area where the person lives for the duration of the barring order for up to three years unless it has been extended beyond that by the Circuit Court. Barring orders are available to:

- A husband or wife who is being subjected to violence, on their own behalf or on behalf of a child
- A civil partner who is being subjected to violence and who has some ownership of the property in question or believes that they have at least an equal legal or beneficial interest in the property concerned
- An abused partner (if a couple is not married and lived together in an intimate relationship prior to the application for the barring order with some ownership of the property or belief of at least an equal legal or beneficial interest in the property in question)
- A parent of a grown child unless the child owns or has greatest ownership of the house
- Tusla, on somebody's behalf.

Protection Orders

A protection order is made until the outcome of a safety order or barring order procedure is known and is only of temporary duration. Under the 2018 act, it may be given in cases where there are reasonable grounds to believe that the safety or welfare of the applicant for the order concerned or of a dependent person so requires. It can be made without the knowledge of the person committing the violence (*ex parte*) where the court considers it necessary or expedient to do so in the interests of justice. However, where such *ex parte* applications are made they must be supported by sworn evidence based on an affidavit or information sworn by the applicant, a copy of which will be served on the respondent (person against whom the order is being made) as soon as is practicable. Such protection order will then cease to have effect on the determination of the application for a safety order or a barring order.

CHAPTER 14

DATA PROTECTION ACTS 1988 TO 2018

Where information is held about a family or child in a childcare setting it is subject to the Data Protection Acts of 1988 to 2018. As the title suggests, this act is based around the original Data Protection Act 1988 but also includes changes made by the Data Protection Act 2018. The 2018 act was passed to bring into effect Regulation (EU) 2016/679 of the European Parliament and of the Council of Europe.

The Data Protection Act 1988 restricts the use of 'personal data', which means 'data relating to a living individual who can be identified either from the data or from the data in conjunction with other information in the possession of the data collector'.

The act states that data collected on a person:

- Should be fairly gained
- Should be accurate and up to date
- Should be kept for only one or more specified lawful purposes
- Shall not be disclosed in other circumstances
- Shall be adequate, relevant and not excessive

- Shall not be kept longer than necessary to fulfil its purposes.

The act also specifies that the person holding the data must have adequate security in place to protect the data and there should be no unauthorised access to the data, which cannot be altered, destroyed or disclosed without the person's permission.

A person is entitled under the act to request to know if such data exists about them and, on the payment of a nominal fee, to have a copy of such data within forty days. Where the information is found to be false or mistaken, the person is entitled to have such errors or mistakes rectified.

A person working with children should always be aware that such a request can be made on behalf of a child in their care, under the Data Protection Act 1988 particularly, and should ensure that information kept is adequate and not excessive for the protection of the best interests of the child. More importantly, childcare workers should respect the privacy and confidentiality of any information given to them in relation to any child in the childcare setting and also be aware that there are fines for breaches of the Data Protection Acts.

Modern life and living intervenes again in relation particularly to the Data Protection Act 2018, which effectively incorporates the General Data Protection Regulations (GDPR) of the European Union. GDPR contains certain elements that strengthen the protection of children's personal data and ensure that the processes used are easily understood by the children themselves so that they can assert their rights personally if required, especially in relation to online services. Children have the right to request a copy of their personal data under both the Data Protection Act 1988 and the Data Protection Act 2018. The competence of the child will be a consideration as it will affect their ability to understand the implications of their decisions in sharing data that relates to them. This concept is further enhanced by the insertion of the age at which a child can consent in relation to what is referred to as the Information Society Services (ISS). The act specifies in Section 8 (which deals with making complaints to the Data Protection Commission) that the age for such consent is sixteen.

Recital 38 of the General Data Protection Guidelines clearly asserts the position of children in relation to data protection:

> Children require special protection with regard to their personal data, as they may be less aware of the risks, consequences and safeguards concerned and their rights in relation to the processing of personal data. Such specific protection should, in particular, apply to the use of personal data of children for the purposes of marketing or creating personality or user profiles and the collection of personal data with regard to children when using services offered directly to a child. The consent of the holder of parental responsibility should

not be necessary in the context of preventive or counselling services offered directly to a child.

It is this special consideration of effective vulnerability of children which is the focus of the protections that should be offered to them and that the Data Protection Act 2018 aims to provide.

Sections 32 provides:

(1)   Without prejudice to the generality of Article 40, the Commission shall encourage the drawing up of codes of conduct intended to contribute to the proper application of the Data Protection Regulation with regard to—

   (a)   the protection of children,

   (b)   the information to be provided by a controller to children,

   (c)   the manner in which the consent of the holders of parental responsibility over a child is to be obtained for the purposes of Article 8,

   (d)   integrating the necessary safeguards into processing in order to protect the rights of children in an age-appropriate manner for the purpose of Article 25,

and

(e)   the processing of the personal data of children for the purposes of direct marketing and creating personality and user profiles.

(2)   For the purpose of considering whether a draft code of conduct or an extension or amendment to an existing code of conduct referred to in Article 40 provides sufficient appropriate safeguards referred to in that Article, the Commission may, where the draft, extension or amendment, as the case may be, concerns the application of the Data Protection Regulation to children, consult with such persons as it considers appropriate including—

(a)   children and bodies who appear to the Commission to represent the interests of children,

(b)   the holders of parental responsibility over children,

and

(c)   the Ombudsman for Children.

Section 33 deals with children's right to be forgotten and provides:

(1)   Subject to *subsection (3)*, in accordance with Article 17, a controller shall, at the request of a data subject, without undue delay erase personal data of the data

subject where the data have been collected in relation to the offer to that data subject of information society services referred to in Article 8(1).

(2)   Subject to *subsection (3)*, where a controller has disclosed the personal data which are the subject of a request under *subsection (1)* to another controller or controllers, the first-mentioned controller shall, taking account of available technology and the cost of implementation, take all reasonable steps, including technical measures, to inform the other controller or controllers which are processing that personal data that the data subject has requested the erasure by such controllers of any links to, or copy or replication of, that personal data.

(3)   *Subsections (1)* and *(2)* shall not apply to the extent that the processing of the personal data concerned is necessary for the purposes set out in Article 17(3).

You may think that these specific measures may not apply to you, but you may be asked to allow children to access online learning, for instance, which may effectively constitute Information Society Services (ISS). In such a case, a child has the right to know these details, bearing in mind their age and level of understanding but always in the pursuit and protection of their best interests. You therefore may have more responsibility than you realise, particularly if you assisted the ISS in obtaining information from the child either intentionally or unwittingly by signing up on behalf of a child in your care.

CHAPTER 15

OMBUDSMAN FOR CHILDREN ACT 2002

The Ombudsman for Children Act 2002 established the post of Ombudsman for Children and provided that such office should be independent. Furthermore, the Ombudsman is charged with performing his or her duty having regard to 'the best interests of the child' concerned and in so far as practicable should give due consideration, having regard to the age and understanding of the child, to his or her wishes. A child under the act is somebody under eighteen years of age, except where the person is enlisted with the Defence Forces.

As this book illustrates, the best interests of the child are central to the protection of children's rights under the Constitution, although these rights are not actually specified. This act also employs the familiar expression 'in so far as is practicable', which basically means that other factors may militate against the application of these ideals.

The act charges the Ombudsman for Children with the promotion of the rights and welfare of children, which includes:

- Advising government ministers on the development and co-ordination of policy relating to children

- Encouraging public bodies, schools and voluntary hospitals to develop policies, practices and procedures designed to promote the rights and welfare of children

- Collecting and disseminating information on matters relating to the rights and welfare of children

- Promoting awareness among members of the public (including children of appropriate age) on matters relating to the rights and welfare of the child, including the UN Convention on the Rights of the Child

- Highlighting issues of concern to children in relation to their rights and welfare

- Co-operating and exchanging information with the Ombudsman for Children (or equivalent post) in other states

- Monitoring and reviewing generally the operation of legislation concerning matters that relate to the rights and welfare of children

- Monitoring and reviewing the operation of the Ombudsman for Children Act 2002.

The ideals of the Convention on the Rights of the Child are very much the starting point of this piece of legislation and the act further charges the Ombudsman with setting up structures to consult regularly with groups of children considered by the Ombudsman to be representative of children. In such consultations the views of the child are to be given due weight in accordance with the age and understanding of the child.

The Ombudsman for Children is appointed by the President after the resolution (agreement) of the Dáil and the Seanad and holds office for a period of six years, which can be renewed once only (i.e. the maximum period that can be served is twelve years). The Ombudsman may be removed from office (at his or her request or for reasons stated in the act) by the President, again on the resolution of both Houses of the Oireachtas.

CHAPTER 16

EDUCATION (WELFARE)
ACT 2000

The Education (Welfare) Act 2000 provides for the entitlement of every child in the State to a certain minimum education (whether that is in a recognised school or otherwise provided, such as home schooling). A minimum standard of education was also set as an ideal in the Constitution under Article 42.2 and in the UN Convention on the Rights of the Child under Articles 28 and 29.

For the purposes of this act, a 'child' refers to 'a person resident in the State who has reached the age of six years and who (*a*) has not reached the age of sixteen years, or (*b*) has not completed three years of post-primary education, whichever occurs later, but shall not include a person who has reached the age of eighteen years'.

The act established the National Educational Welfare Board, which is charged with the implementation of the detail of the act. The act sets out the functions of the National Educational Welfare Board (NEWB) as follows:

(a) to promote and foster in society, and in particular in families, an appreciation of the benefits to be derived from education, in particular as respects the physical, intellectual, emotional, social, cultural and moral development of children, and of the social and economic advantages that flow therefrom,

(b) to promote and foster, in recognised schools, an environment that encourages children to attend school and participate fully in the life of the school,

(c) to conduct and commission research into the reasons for non-attendance on the part of students and into strategies and programmes designed to prevent it,

(d) to disseminate to recognised schools the findings of research conducted or commissioned pursuant to paragraph (c), and to advise such schools on matters relating to the prevention of non-attendance, and the good conduct of students generally,

(e) to assist recognised schools in so far as is practicable to meet their obligations under this act,

(f) to advise and assist children and the parents of children who exhibit problems relating to attendance at, and behaviour in, school,

(g) to support, monitor, and assess the effectiveness of, strategies and programmes aimed at preventing non-attendance in recognised schools,

(h)   to co-operate with such persons as the Board considers appropriate, and to co-ordinate the activities of the Board with the activities of those persons in so far as they relate to preventing non-attendance in recognised schools,

(i)   to carry out reviews of training and guidance given to teachers relating to matters of school attendance and the conduct of students, and to advise the Minister in relation thereto,

(j)   to advise the National Council for Curriculum and Assessment as respects those aspects of the school curriculum that, in the opinion of the Board, are likely to have an effect on attendance levels at, or the extent of student participation in, school, and

(k)   to advise the Minister on any matter to which this Act relates.

Interestingly, the act requires the National Educational Welfare Board to have due regard to the cost of the measures it proposes, which could be interpreted as putting a financial limit on the best interests of the child.

Behavioural aspects in school form a part of the act's provisions, and in situations where behaviour may indicate other underlying problems, the act allows for investigations to take place in relation to that behaviour. The National Educational Welfare

Board can, with the agreement of parents, arrange for a child to be assessed. Where such consent is not given by the parents, the board can apply to the Circuit Court for an order that the assessment takes place where the Circuit Court agrees that it appears necessary for such assessment to take place.

The act allows for the appointment of educational welfare officers, who are appointed by warrant which can be produced when exercising their functions (again in keeping with the ideals expressed in both the Irish Constitution and the UN Convention on the Rights of the Child). The board can assign additional functions to such officers outside of those specified in the act.

The act requires a register to be kept of every child who is receiving education other than in a recognised establishment and to have that standard ascertained to ensure that the child in question is receiving a minimum standard of education. Where this is not the case, the standard must be increased.

It does not state that this requirement is in the child's best interests, and indeed the child may by definition require much more than the minimum (particularly if the child is gifted or talented), but this is not dealt with in the act even though it could affect the child's performance, attendance and behaviour.

The act provides that parents or guardians must ensure that where children do attend recognised schools they must attend regularly and that in the case of unwarranted absences parents can be held liable for non-attendance, which can mean a fine and/or imprisonment.

CHAPTER 17

EDUCATION FOR PERSONS WITH SPECIAL EDUCATIONAL NEEDS ACT 2004

The Education for Persons with Special Educational Needs Act 2004 (also known as the EPSEN Act) is a very important step in realising the goal of equality in relation to education for people with special needs. The act also provided for the setting up of the National Council for Special Education and set out how decisions may be appealed. The act had not been fully implemented when it was effectively suspended by the 2008 Budget – the aim was to bring the act into operation over ten years but this, while not negated, has been frustrated or delayed.

The act states that 'special educational needs' refers to 'a restriction in the capacity of the person to participate in and benefit from education on account of an enduring physical, sensory, mental health or learning disability, or any other condition which results in a person learning differently from a person without that condition'. The act provides that

> A child with special educational needs shall be educated in an inclusive environment with children who do not have such needs unless

the nature or degree of those needs of the child is such that to do so would be inconsistent with—

(a)   the best interests of the child as determined in accordance with any assessment carried out under this act, or

(b)   the effective provision of education for children with whom the child is to be educated.

It should be noted that this is a provision with a tail – in other words, exceptions can be made to inclusive education, specifically where it might interfere with a child's ability to participate where that child has no special need.

The act puts responsibility on a school principal where the parents inform the principal that they are of the opinion that the child is not benefiting as much as would be expected from what is being offered in the school or where the principal forms this view and may believe that this is because the child may have special needs. In such cases, the principal must arrange to have the student assessed within a month of forming that view. The assessment must be completed within three months of the formation of the view (in other words, within two months of the start of the plan). Guidelines for such assessment will be provided by the National Council for Special Education.

If the child is assessed as having special needs (the act specifies who would be suitably qualified to carry out such an assessment), the principal must have a plan prepared for the appropriate education of that child within one month of receiving this confirmation. This plan is called an Individual Educational Plan or IEP for the child. It must be drawn up in consultation with the parents and teachers if appropriate. The principal must give written notice of such a plan to the parents and give them a copy of the plan.

In the case of a child whose special needs are such that an IEP prepared by the school would not meet the needs of the child or where an IEP already prepared is not meeting the needs of the child, the principal must request the National Council for Special Education to prepare an education plan.

Tusla may also arrange an assessment of a child where it forms the view that the child may have special needs whether a student or not.

It is a requirement that parents be consulted throughout this process, but where parents refuse to agree to an assessment the Circuit Court may do so in the best interests of the child.

The plan should include:

- The type and extent of the child's abilities, skills and talents
- The type and extent of the child's special educational needs and how they affect the child's educational development
- The level of the child's current educational performance

- The child's special educational needs (what could be offered in such cases)
- The supports needed to ensure that the child benefits from education
- Where necessary, the supports the child needs to make the change from pre-school to primary school
- Similarly, the supports the child needs to make the move from primary to secondary school
- The goals the child should achieve over a period of not more than one year.

The principal is responsible for putting the prepared plan into action. The principal must review the plan at least once a year to ensure that the services specified in the plan were received and the goals of the plan were met. If the parents feel that a review is necessary and one has not taken place in the previous six months, they may request that a review be done, and the principal must inform the parents if one is not done. The act also specifies that if the child moves school, then the principal must let the principal of the new school know that a plan exists before a transfer takes place.

Childcare workers should be aware that a child may have an IEP in place and activities undertaken in relation to that child should follow the procedures, methods and goals of the plan. Such children have a right to expect that all people working with them are aware of and follow their IEP.

Once again, the value of observation is important in this regard as not everybody will inform you about the fact that a child may have a 'special need', and indeed you may be the first to observe the need for a possible assessment of such special need.

CHAPTER 18

DISABILITY ACT 2005

The Disability Act 2005 defines a disability in relation to a person as meaning:

> . . . a substantial restriction in the capacity of the person, which is permanent or likely to be permanent, to carry on a profession, business or occupation in the State or to participate in social or cultural life in the State by reason of an enduring physical, sensory, mental health or intellectual impairment.

The act provides similar provisions to those that apply in the Education for Persons with Special Educational Needs Act 2004 but there is an Assessment of Need Report rather than an IEP.

The Assessment of Need Report will include:

- Whether a person has a disability
- The nature and extent of the disability
- The health and education needs arising from the disability
- The services considered appropriate to meet those needs and the timescale ideally required for their delivery
- When a review of assessment should take place.

The person with the disability will be involved with the process and in some cases Tusla can initiate the assessment on behalf of a person.

Children with a disability can be assessed under the Disability Act 2005 or under the Education for Persons with Special Educational Needs Act 2004 as there may be special needs as a result of the disability. Where this happens, the National Council for Special Education or the principal of the school the child attends is notified of that aspect of the assessment.

The Disability Act 2005 also stipulates appeal procedures where a person is not satisfied with the procedure, and these are heard by a complaints officer.

The act also:

- Provides that people with disabilities should have access to public buildings, services and information
- Establishes sectoral plans for six government departments to ensure that services for people with disabilities are integrated into planning and provision
- Establishes a duty on public bodies to be proactive in employing people with disabilities
- Prohibits the use of genetic testing for employment, mortgage or insurance purposes
- Establishes a Centre for Excellence in Universal Design.

One possible flaw with the act is that while it says equality of access should be available for persons with disability, it excludes some places where it is considered not to be practicable or justifiable on cost grounds or where there would be unreasonable delay in doing so. This may, however, exclude people on the basis of cost or delay and it does not say who would judge whether such an exception would be reasonable.

There is at last a commitment by the Irish State to ensure that the provisions of the United Nations Convention on the Rights of Persons with a Disability are met and this will change the landscape particularly in relation to children.

CHAPTER 19

UNITED NATIONS CONVENTION ON THE RIGHTS OF PERSONS WITH A DISABILITY

The United Nations Convention on the Rights of Persons with Disabilities (CRPD) was adopted on 13 December 2006 in New York. Eighty-two countries signed the Convention and one country ratified it. Ratification means that they included it in their laws and it had immediate effect. The Convention came into force on 3 May 2008. Interestingly, Ireland, having signed the Convention in 2007 (meaning it promised to move towards ratification by changing its laws until all the elements of the Convention were in place), only finally ratified it in March 2018.

As with other conventions, there is an operating protocol attached to the CRPD which outlines how complaints will be handled, who they will be handled by and who will assist in the process. Therefore, a clear process and procedures are outlined, which come into effect as soon as possible after ratification by any country.

In Section (f) of the Preamble of the CRPD there is a recollection of the UN Convention on the Rights of the Child (UNCRC), which indicates that this convention takes into account the UNCRC and therefore has within its aims the protection of the best interests of the child, as previously outlined.

Article 1 of the UNCRPD outlines its purpose as follows:

> The purpose of the present Convention is to promote, protect and ensure the full and equal enjoyment of all human rights and fundamental freedoms by all persons with disabilities, and to promote respect for their inherent dignity.
>
> Persons with disabilities include those who have long-term physical, mental, intellectual or sensory impairments which in interaction with various barriers may hinder their full and effective participation in society on an equal basis with others.

Article 3 of the CRPD outlines its principles as follows:

(a)   Respect for inherent dignity, individual autonomy including the freedom to make one's own choices, and independence of persons;

(b)   Non-discrimination;

(c)   Full and effective participation and inclusion in society;

(d)   Respect for difference and acceptance of persons with disabilities as part of human diversity and humanity;

(e)   Equality of opportunity;

(f)   Accessibility;

(g)   Equality between men and women;

(h)   Respect for the evolving capacities of children with disabilities and respect for the right of children with disabilities to preserve their identities.

Article 5 states in relation to 'equality and non-discrimination' that:

1.   States Parties recognize that all persons are equal before and under the law and are entitled without any discrimination to the equal protection and equal benefit of the law.

2.   States Parties shall prohibit all discrimination on the basis of disability and guarantee to persons with disabilities equal and effective legal protection against discrimination on all grounds.

3.   In order to promote equality and eliminate discrimination, States Parties shall take all appropriate steps to ensure that reasonable accommodation is provided.

4.   Specific measures which are necessary to accelerate or achieve de facto equality of persons with disabilities shall not be considered discrimination under the terms of the present Convention.

In other words, for somebody caring, working or representing people with a disability under the CRPD, the State should provide reasonable accommodation, defined in the CRPD as

necessary and appropriate modification and adjustments not imposing a disproportionate or undue burden, where needed in a particular case, to ensure to persons with disabilities the enjoyment or exercise on an equal basis with others of all human rights and fundamental freedoms.

The CRPD is therefore clearly based on the concept that people (which includes children) should have a full and sustaining life that takes account of any challenges the person is faced with and that the State will assist as far as it can without undue burden to support the ideals of equality and non-discrimination as far as possible in legislation.

Article 7 is specifically concerned with children with disabilities and outlines:

1.   States Parties shall take all necessary measures to ensure the full enjoyment by children with disabilities of all human rights and fundamental freedoms on an equal basis with other children.

2.   In all actions concerning children with disabilities, the best interests of the child shall be a primary consideration.

3.   States Parties shall ensure that children with disabilities have the right to express their views freely on all matters affecting them, their views being given due weight in accordance with their age and maturity, on an equal basis with other children, and to be provided with disability and age-appropriate assistance to realize that right.

The concept is clearly outlined in paragraph 2 above, where it says that 'the best interests of the child shall be a primary consideration', and this paragraph 3 outlines that children with disabilities are 'to be provided with disability and age-appropriate assistance to realise that right'. Where a child with a disability is within your care, it is part of your role to ensure the child gets any assistance needed to ensure their best interests are provided for. That is the child's right and your duty.

CHAPTER 20

CRIMINAL JUSTICE ACT 2006

As can be expected in any society, there are occasions when children in Ireland find themselves on the wrong side of the law. The Criminal Justice Act 2006 has made significant changes to the way such instances are dealt with.

This 2006 act changed the age of criminal responsibility in relation to a child to twelve (except in the case of murder, manslaughter, rape or aggravated assault when a child is aged ten or eleven). It directs that in its dealings 'with a child charged with an offence, a court shall have due regard to the child's best interests, the interests of the victim of the offence and the protection of society'. Here we see that a triangulated view of the best interests of the child is taken, and indeed throughout the act the use of the phrase 'best interests of the child' is sparse, to say the least.

Many of the measures included in the act are new to the Irish situation, for example behaviour orders, and the wording in these sections is based on a belief that children must accept responsibility for their actions and agree to change the behaviour that caused the problem.

The act provides for assistance to be given to children in relation to legal proceedings against them, and states that where they are detained they should be detained separately from adults (as would be the case in St Patrick's Institution, for instance), except where it would not be in the child's best interests to do so.

While the wording of the act may be terse, as one might expect in relation to criminal matters, the concepts outlined in the Convention on the Rights of the Child are present, such as children's rights to representation, to timely administration of justice, to challenge their detention and to have matters they raise dealt with by an impartial authority.

The notion of 'evolving capacities' is also incorporated into the act in Section 124, which provides:

> Where a child under 14 years of age is charged with an offence, the Court may, of its own motion or the application of any person, dismiss the case on its merits if, having had due regard to the child's age and level of maturity, it determines that the child did not have a full understanding of what was involved in the commission of the offence.

CHAPTER 21

CHILD CARE (AMENDMENT) ACT 2007

The Child Care (Amendment) Act 2007 relates to children who have been in the care of the same foster or relative family for five years or more. It might appear on first reading that this is similar to the Adoption Act 1988; however, it differs significantly in that it does not relate to adoption by the people who have been looking after the child but rather puts them in the parental role where that is in the child's best interests.

The courts can make an order to allow the qualifying relative or foster parent

(a)   to have, on behalf of Tusla, the like control over the child as if the foster parent or relative were the child's parent, and

(b)   to do, on behalf of Tusla, what is reasonable (subject to the provisions of this Act and of the regulations for the time being in force under this Act) in all the circumstances of the case for the purpose of safeguarding and promoting the child's health, development or welfare and, in particular, give consent to—

(i)   any necessary medical or psychiatric examination, treatment or assessment with respect to the child, and

(ii)   the issue of a passport to, or the provision of passport facilities for, the child to enable the child to travel abroad for a limited period.

Under the act the courts must be satisfied that:

(a)   the foster parent or relative has been taking care of the child for a period of not less than five years beginning on the date of placement in accordance with this Act and ending on the date of application,

(b)   the granting of the order is in the child's best interests,

(c)   Tusla has consented in advance to the granting of the order,

(d)   Tusla has, on behalf of the foster parent or relative—

(i)   if the child is in its care under section 4, obtained the consent to the granting of the order of a parent having custody of the child at the relevant time or of a person (other than the foster parent or relative) acting *in loco parentis* to the child, or

(ii)   if the child is in its care under section 18, given notice of the application to a parent having custody of the child at the relevant time or of a person (other than the foster parent or relative) acting *in loco parentis* to the child, and

(e)   the child's wishes have, in so far as is practicable, been given due consideration having regard to the age and understanding of the child.

The act provides that the consent of the parent included above does not apply if:

(a)   the court is satisfied that he or she is missing and cannot be found by Tusla, or

(b)   the court, having regard to the child's welfare, so directs.

An order under the act can be conditional and can be reversed (as outlined in the act), which is where the central difference between this act and the Adoption Act 1988 lies. The purpose of placing the temporary carer in the position of the parent in the Child Care (Amendment) Act 2007 is to allow permission to be given for medical treatment, including but not restricted to psychiatric treatment. Similarly, it would never be in the child's best interests to be the only child in a whole school not to go on a foreign trip, for instance, just because the foster parents or foster relatives could not provide the necessary permissions needed to get a passport to travel out of the country.

CHAPTER 22

PASSPORT ACT 2008

The Passport Act 2008 allows the Minister for Foreign Affairs to authorise the issuing of a passport to a child where the minister is 'satisfied on reasonable grounds that each person who is a guardian of the child consents to the issue of a passport to the child'. This act has been updated and while the base act (2008) is still obvious, there are significant changes in relation to gender changes that may be undertaken and may give rise to difficulties in relation to the new gender of passport applicants.

There are often situations where the issuing of a passport for a child can prove problematic and the Passport Act 2008 tries to include those situations. Again the issue of new family groupings can create issues that need to be addressed within what were prior established situations such as the issuing of passports. In this regard, an adjustment to Section 14 of the Passport Act 2008 was applied following the Children and Family Relationships Act 2015 as follows:

(1)   Subject to this section, the Minister shall, before issuing a passport to a child, be satisfied on reasonable grounds that –

(a) where the child has 2 guardians, each guardian of the child, and

(b) where the child has more than 2 guardians, not fewer than 2 of those guardians,

consents to the issue of a passport to the child.

The act allows the Minister for Foreign Affairs on the application of only one guardian to issue a passport for a child where perhaps one parent lives abroad with the child:

(a) having regard to all the circumstances of the case, including whether or not that other guardian of the child has notified the Minister in writing that he or she objects to the issue of a passport to the child, and

(b) for the purpose of securing the welfare of the child

This provision might be used to facilitate the return of the child or assist in proceedings to have the child repatriated in some situations.

The minister can also issue a passport with the consent of one guardian, or indeed no guardian, where the application is made by somebody who has an interest in the welfare of the child and the minister is satisfied:

(a) there exist in relation to the child exceptional circumstances involving an immediate and serious risk of harm to his or her life, health or safety requiring him or her to undertake travel for which a passport is required, and

(b)   for the purpose of securing the welfare of the child.

Additionally, it may be the case that the minister agrees to the issue of a passport on the basis of a court order from another country which has been legitimately obtained and which is in the child's best interests.

All these conditions could be seen as facilitating children to have access to their family and indeed to their nationality and identity as required under the Convention on the Rights of the Child. The ability of the minister to put the child's welfare above the guardian's permission may be essential in some situations where families are scattered throughout the world but such situations would be dealt with on an individual case basis.

The act states that guardians who give their permission will be taken to have agreed indefinitely unless they communicate their change of mind to the minister in writing. This avoids any difficulties which might arise if a relevant guardian were to lose contact with the child for any number of reasons.

CHAPTER 23

CHILDREN AND FAMILY RELATIONSHIPS ACT 2015

The effects of the Children and Family Relationships Act 2015 have been seen throughout this book. One of the most all-encompassing acts of the past one hundred years, it offers a fantastic protection to the best interest of the child in its goal to address the changing nature of life today.

Part 2 of the act deals with issues in relation to the process of Donor Assisted Human Reproduction (DAHR) particularly in relation to parentage, permissions (before, during and after the process), access to information, recognitions and processes, with the intention of protecting those who take part in DAHR and those who are the result of those processes.

Part 3 outlines the duties and responsibilities of those who carry out the processes of DAHR, registration of such activities and procedures for the carrying out of legal DAHR.

Part 4 deals with Amendments to the Guardianship of Infants Act 1964, in particular who is and can be the guardian of children in different situations.

Part 5 deals with amendments to the Succession Act 1965, which has significant relevance to children's future succession rights in whatever type of family they are deemed to be under the law.

Part 6 deals with amendments to the Family Law (Maintenance of Spouses and Children) Act 1987 so that children and adults are properly maintained in whatever family situation arises in their lives.

Part 7 deals with Amendments to the Status of Children Act 1987, which has already been covered in this book.

Part 8 deals with amendments to the Family Law Act 1995 and outlines the legal elements in relation to families such as cohabitants.

Part 9 deals with amendments to the Civil Registration Act 2004, covering the civil registration of family relationships that already exist, such as the registration of the birth of donor conceived children and what it is to be a parent of a donor-conceived child.

Part 10 deals with amendments to the Passport Act 2010, which sets out the issues that could arise in relation to the permissions necessary for the issuing of a passport, particularly in relation to children in different family types and family relationship situations.

Part 11 deals with amendments to the Adoption Act 2010, which covers parents, fathers, mothers, cohabiting partners and guardians of children, second mothers, second fathers, step parents and relatives, which has become a very complicated part of family relationships in Ireland and abroad.

Part 12 deals with amendments to Civil Partnership and Certain Rights and Obligations of Cohabitants Act 2010, which provides within its elements the provision for civil and financial elements of cohabiting.

CHAPTER 24

THE BEST INTERESTS OF THE CHILD

As this book has illustrated, the expression 'the best interests of the child' is widely used and is a fundamental concept in the treatment of children in the Irish legal system under legislation and within the protections for children provided for in our Constitution, and indeed under the UN Convention on the Rights of the Child. However, it is just an expression; to have true effect, it must be given meaning in practice.

It is useful to note that the word 'interests' is plural but the word 'child' is singular. It reminds us to relate to the child as an individual and not as part of a group setting. Each situation must be dealt with individually and the solutions found should take account of each individual child.

The child must be put at the centre of decisions made concerning him or her to achieve the best possible outcome in relation to that child. In so far as possible, that child must be allowed to express his or her opinion in relation to such deliberations according to his or her 'evolving capacities' as stated in the Convention on the Rights of the Child. Conceivably, this also means that the solution should be reviewed as the child evolves – an interesting concept not yet addressed in the Irish system (with the possible exception of the Mental Health Act).

The concept of the best decision in relation to the individual child was investigated by a South African Constitutional Court judge, Albie Sachs, in the case of *M v. The State* (Case CCT 53/06 [2007] ZACC18). Judge Sachs had to decide on an option of the courts in South Africa to jail a mother over repeated fraud offences despite leniency of sentencing in previous cases. The judge held that in the circumstances of the mother's children and their best interests, it was not appropriate to activate a jail sentence for the woman as her children might be put at risk, and that a more appropriate punishment would be community service where the mother could still look after her children and thus protect their interests.

Scotland's Commissioner for Children and Young People, Kathleen Marshall, also examined this topic in a report published in February 2008, called *Not Seen. Not Heard. Not Guilty. The Rights and Status of the Children of Prisoners in Scotland*. The report considered the effect on children when a parent is imprisoned and pointed out that it did not always have a negative impact, as in some cases the child might be relieved that the parent has been imprisoned and may feel safer as a result. It is clear that there is no one-size-fits-all solution; rather a consideration of all elements of the individual child's life should be taken into account when decisions are made. Indeed, Marshall pointed out that this is not always easy either, as when some children feel vulnerable it can be hard to ascertain their views and 'children will often tell ChildLine things they would not tell anyone else'.

To secure the best interests of the child we must take a child-centred approach to all dealings with children. In the words of Judge Sachs:

> ... every child has his or her own dignity. If a child is to be constitutionally imagined as an individual with a distinctive personality, and not merely as a miniature adult waiting to reach full size, he or she cannot be treated as a mere extension of his or her parents, umbilically destined to sink or swim with them.

A child-centred focus allows the child to grow into the best possible adult he or she is capable of being and this requires some assistance along the way from the people who come into contact with that child in whatever capacity.

As a person working with children, you must be aware of the effect of every aspect of your behaviour on the children in your care. You must listen to the opinions of the children in your care and give due consideration to those opinions, bearing in mind the child's evolving capacities, and you must provide a voice for children who cannot articulate for themselves. In every aspect of your work you are charged with the protection of the children in your care from abuse, neglect and exploitation. You are also responsible for ensuring that each child in your care develops to his or her best potential in a safe and nurturing environment, bearing in mind the words of Judge Sachs:

> Individually and collectively all children have the right to express themselves as independent social beings, to have their own laughter as well as sorrow, to play, to imagine and explore in their own way, to themselves get to understand their bodies, minds and emotions, and above all to learn as they grow how they should conduct themselves and make choices in the wide social and moral world of adulthood. And foundational to the enjoyment of the right to childhood is the promotion of the right as far as possible to live in a secure and nurturing environment free from violence, fear, want and avoidable trauma.

A child who smiles unconditionally, asks questions without fear, enjoys life to the full and strives with the help of others to reach their best potential, is one of the future custodians of our world. The job done by those who work with children to achieve this goal takes courage, dedication, empathy, resilience and fortitude, especially in the face of the many challenges of childhood today. Protecting the child's best interests in this process is an invaluable role undertaken by a select few for the benefit of all.

APPENDIX 1

Convention on the Rights of the Child

Adopted and opened for signature, ratification and accession by General Assembly resolution 44/25 of 20 November 1989

Entry into force 2 September 1990, in accordance with article 49

Preamble

The States Parties to the present Convention,

Considering that, in accordance with the principles proclaimed in the Charter of the United Nations, recognition of the inherent dignity and of the equal and inalienable rights of all members of the human family is the foundation of freedom, justice and peace in the world,

Bearing in mind that the peoples of the United Nations have, in the Charter, reaffirmed their faith in fundamental human rights and in the dignity and worth of the human person, and have determined to promote social progress and better standards of life in larger freedom,

Recognizing that the United Nations has, in the Universal Declaration of Human Rights and in the International Covenants on Human Rights, proclaimed and agreed that everyone is entitled to all the rights and freedoms set forth therein, without distinction of any kind, such as race, colour, sex, language, religion, political or other opinion, national or social origin, property, birth or other status,

Recalling that, in the Universal Declaration of Human Rights, the United Nations has proclaimed that childhood is entitled to special care and assistance,

Convinced that the family, as the fundamental group of society and the natural environment for the growth and well-being of all its members and particularly children, should be afforded the necessary protection and assistance so that it can fully assume its responsibilities within the community,

Recognizing that the child, for the full and harmonious development of his or her personality, should grow up in a family environment, in an atmosphere of happiness, love and understanding,

Considering that the child should be fully prepared to live an individual life in society, and brought up in the spirit of the ideals proclaimed in the Charter of the United Nations, and in particular in the spirit of peace, dignity, tolerance, freedom, equality and solidarity,

Bearing in mind that the need to extend particular care to the child has been stated in the Geneva Declaration of the Rights of the Child of 1924 and in the Declaration of the Rights of the Child adopted by the General Assembly on 20 November 1959 and recognized in the Universal Declaration of Human Rights, in the International Covenant on Civil and Political Rights (in particular in articles 23 and 24), in the International Covenant on Economic, Social and Cultural Rights (in particular in article 10) and in the statutes and relevant instruments of specialized agencies and international organizations concerned with the welfare of children,

Bearing in mind that, as indicated in the Declaration of the Rights of the Child, 'the child, by reason of his physical and mental immaturity, needs special safeguards and care, including appropriate legal protection, before as well as after birth',

Recalling the provisions of the Declaration on Social and Legal Principles relating to the Protection and Welfare of Children, with Special Reference to Foster Placement and Adoption Nationally and Internationally; the United Nations Standard Minimum Rules for the Administration of Juvenile Justice (The Beijing Rules); and the Declaration on the Protection of Women and Children in Emergency and Armed Conflict,

Recognizing that, in all countries in the world, there are children living in exceptionally difficult conditions, and that such children need special consideration,

Taking due account of the importance of the traditions and cultural values of each people for the protection and harmonious development of the child,

Recognizing the importance of international co-operation for improving the living conditions of children in every country, in particular in the developing countries,

Have agreed as follows:

Part I

Article 1

For the purposes of the present Convention, a child means every human being below the age of eighteen years unless under the law applicable to the child, majority is attained earlier.

Article 2

1. States Parties shall respect and ensure the rights set forth in the present Convention to each child within their jurisdiction without discrimination of any kind, irrespective of the child's or his or her parent's or legal guardian's race, colour, sex, language, religion, political or other opinion, national, ethnic or social origin, property, disability, birth or other status.

2. States Parties shall take all appropriate measures to ensure that the child is protected against all forms of discrimination or punishment on the basis of the status, activities, expressed opinions, or beliefs of the child's parents, legal guardians, or family members.

Article 3

1. In all actions concerning children, whether undertaken by public or private social welfare institutions, courts of law, administrative authorities or legislative bodies, the best interests of the child shall be a primary consideration.

2. States Parties undertake to ensure the child such protection and care as is necessary for his or her

well-being, taking into account the rights and duties of his or her parents, legal guardians, or other individuals legally responsible for him or her, and, to this end, shall take all appropriate legislative and administrative measures.

3. States Parties shall ensure that the institutions, services and facilities responsible for the care or protection of children shall conform with the standards established by competent authorities, particularly in the areas of safety, health, in the number and suitability of their staff, as well as competent supervision.

Article 4

States Parties shall undertake all appropriate legislative, administrative, and other measures for the implementation of the rights recognized in the present Convention. With regard to economic, social and cultural rights, States Parties shall undertake such measures to the maximum extent of their available resources and, where needed, within the framework of international co-operation.

Article 5

States Parties shall respect the responsibilities, rights and duties of parents or, where applicable, the members of the extended family or community as provided for by local custom, legal guardians or other persons legally responsible for the child, to provide, in a manner consistent with the evolving capacities of the child, appropriate direction and guidance in the exercise by the child of the rights recognized in the present Convention.

Article 6

1. States Parties recognize that every child has the inherent right to life.

2. States Parties shall ensure to the maximum extent possible the survival and development of the child.

Article 7

1. The child shall be registered immediately after birth and shall have the right from birth to a name, the right to acquire a nationality and, as far as possible, the right to know and be cared for by his or her parents.

2. States Parties shall ensure the implementation of these rights in accordance with their national law and their obligations under the relevant international instruments in this field, in particular where the child would otherwise be stateless.

Article 8

1. States Parties undertake to respect the right of the child to preserve his or her identity, including nationality, name and family relations as recognized by law without unlawful interference.

2. Where a child is illegally deprived of some or all of the elements of his or her identity, States Parties shall provide appropriate assistance and protection, with a view to re-establishing speedily his or her identity.

Article 9

1. States Parties shall ensure that a child shall not be separated from his or her parents against their will, except when competent authorities subject to judicial review determine, in accordance with applicable law and procedures, that such separation is necessary for the best interests of the child. Such determination may be necessary in a particular case such as one involving abuse or neglect of the child by the parents, or one where the parents are living separately and a decision must be made as to the child's place of residence.

2. In any proceedings pursuant to paragraph 1 of the present article, all interested parties shall be given an opportunity to participate in the proceedings and make their views known.

3. States Parties shall respect the right of the child who is separated from one or both parents to maintain personal relations and direct contact with both parents on a regular basis, except if it is contrary to the child's best interests.

4. Where such separation results from any action initiated by a State Party, such as the detention, imprisonment, exile, deportation or death (including death arising from any cause while the person is in the custody of the State) of one or both parents or of the child, that State Party shall, upon request, provide the parents, the child or, if appropriate, another member of the family with the essential information concerning the whereabouts of the absent member(s) of the family unless the provision of the information would be

detrimental to the well-being of the child. States Parties shall further ensure that the submission of such a request shall of itself entail no adverse consequences for the person(s) concerned.

Article 10

1. In accordance with the obligation of States Parties under article 9, paragraph 1, applications by a child or his or her parents to enter or leave a State Party for the purpose of family reunification shall be dealt with by States Parties in a positive, humane and expeditious manner. States Parties shall further ensure that the submission of such a request shall entail no adverse consequences for the applicants and for the members of their family.

2. A child whose parents reside in different States shall have the right to maintain on a regular basis, save in exceptional circumstances personal relations and direct contacts with both parents. Towards that end and in accordance with the obligation of States Parties under article 9, paragraph 1, States Parties shall respect the right of the child and his or her parents to leave any country, including their own, and to enter their own country. The right to leave any country shall be subject only to such restrictions as are prescribed by law and which are necessary to protect the national security, public order (order public), public health or morals or the rights and freedoms of others and are consistent with the other rights recognized in the present Convention.

Article 11

1. States Parties shall take measures to combat the illicit transfer and non-return of children abroad.

2. To this end, States Parties shall promote the conclusion of bilateral or multilateral agreements or accession to existing agreements.

Article 12

1. States Parties shall assure to the child who is capable of forming his or her own views the right to express those views freely in all matters affecting the child, the views of the child being given due weight in accordance with the age and maturity of the child.

2. For this purpose, the child shall in particular be provided the opportunity to be heard in any judicial and administrative proceedings affecting the child, either directly, or through a representative or an appropriate body, in a manner consistent with the procedural rules of national law.

Article 13

1. The child shall have the right to freedom of expression; this right shall include freedom to seek, receive and impart information and ideas of all kinds, regardless of frontiers, either orally, in writing or in print, in the form of art, or through any other media of the child's choice.

2. The exercise of this right may be subject to certain restrictions, but these shall only be such as are provided by law and are necessary:

(a) For respect of the rights or reputations of others; or

(b) For the protection of national security or of public order (order public), or of public health or morals.

Article 14

1. States Parties shall respect the right of the child to freedom of thought, conscience and religion.

2. States Parties shall respect the rights and duties of the parents and, when applicable, legal guardians, to provide direction to the child in the exercise of his or her right in a manner consistent with the evolving capacities of the child.

3. Freedom to manifest one's religion or beliefs may be subject only to such limitations as are prescribed by law and are necessary to protect public safety, order, health or morals, or the fundamental rights and freedoms of others.

Article 15

1. States Parties recognize the rights of the child to freedom of association and to freedom of peaceful assembly.

2. No restrictions may be placed on the exercise of these rights other than those imposed in conformity with the law and which are necessary in a democratic society in the interests of national security or public safety, public order (order public), the protection of public health or morals or the protection of the rights and freedoms of others.

Article 16

1. No child shall be subjected to arbitrary or unlawful interference with his or her privacy, family, home or correspondence, nor to unlawful attacks on his or her honour and reputation.

2. The child has the right to the protection of the law against such interference or attacks.

Article 17

States Parties recognize the important function performed by the mass media and shall ensure that the child has access to information and material from a diversity of national and international sources especially those aimed at the promotion of his or her social, spiritual and moral well-being and physical and mental health.

To this end, States Parties shall:

(a) Encourage the mass media to disseminate information and material of social and cultural benefit to the child and in accordance with the spirit of article 29;

(b) Encourage international co-operation in the production, exchange and dissemination of such information and material from a diversity of cultural, national and international sources;

(c) Encourage the production and dissemination of children's books;

(d) Encourage the mass media to have particular regard to the linguistic needs of the child who belongs to a minority group or who is indigenous;

(e) Encourage the development of appropriate guidelines for the protection of the child from information and material injurious to his or her well-being, bearing in mind the provisions of articles 13 and 18.

Article 18

1. States Parties shall use their best efforts to ensure recognition of the principle that both parents have common responsibilities for the upbringing and development of the child. Parents or, as the case may be, legal guardians, have the primary responsibility for the upbringing and development of the child. The best interests of the child will be their basic concern.

2. For the purpose of guaranteeing and promoting the rights set forth in the present Convention, States Parties shall render appropriate assistance to parents and legal guardians in the performance of their child-rearing responsibilities and shall ensure the development of institutions, facilities and services for the care of children.

3. States Parties shall take all appropriate measures to ensure that children of working parents have the right to benefit from childcare services and facilities for which they are eligible.

Article 19

1. States Parties shall take all appropriate legislative, administrative, social and educational measures to protect the child from all forms of physical or mental violence, injury or abuse, neglect or

negligent treatment, maltreatment or exploitation, including sexual abuse, while in the care of parent(s), legal guardian(s) or any other person who has the care of the child.

2. Such protective measures should, as appropriate, include effective procedures for the establishment of social programmes to provide necessary support for the child and for those who have the care of the child, as well as for other forms of prevention and for identification, reporting, referral, investigation, treatment and follow-up of instances of child maltreatment described heretofore, and, as appropriate, for judicial involvement.

Article 20

1. A child temporarily or permanently deprived of his or her family environment, or in whose own best interests cannot be allowed to remain in that environment, shall be entitled to special protection and assistance provided by the State.

2. States Parties shall in accordance with their national laws ensure alternative care for such a child.

3. Such care could include, inter alia, foster placement, kafalah of Islamic law, adoption or if necessary placement in suitable institutions for the care of children. When considering solutions, due regard shall be paid to the desirability of continuity in a child's upbringing and to the child's ethnic, religious, cultural and linguistic background.

Article 21

States Parties that recognize and/or permit the system of adoption shall ensure that the best interests of the child shall be the paramount consideration and they shall:

(a) Ensure that the adoption of a child is authorized only by competent authorities who determine, in accordance with applicable law and procedures and on the basis of all pertinent and reliable information, that the adoption is permissible in view of the child's status concerning parents, relatives and legal guardians and that, if required, the persons concerned have given their informed consent to the adoption on the basis of such counselling as may be necessary;

(b) Recognize that inter-country adoption may be considered as an alternative means of child's care, if the child cannot be placed in a foster or an adoptive family or cannot in any suitable manner be cared for in the child's country of origin;

(c) Ensure that the child concerned by inter-country adoption enjoys safeguards and standards equivalent to those existing in the case of national adoption;

(d) Take all appropriate measures to ensure that, in inter-country adoption, the placement does not result in improper financial gain for those involved in it;

(e) Promote, where appropriate, the objectives of the present article by concluding bilateral or multilateral arrangements or agreements, and endeavour, within this framework, to ensure that the placement of the child in another country is carried out by competent authorities or organs.

Article 22

1. States Parties shall take appropriate measures to ensure that a child who is seeking refugee status or who is considered a refugee in accordance with applicable international or domestic law and procedures shall, whether unaccompanied or accompanied by his or her parents or by any other person, receive appropriate protection and humanitarian assistance in the enjoyment of applicable rights set forth in the present Convention and in other international human rights or humanitarian instruments to which the said States are Parties.

2. For this purpose, States Parties shall provide, as they consider appropriate, co-operation in any efforts by the United Nations and other competent intergovernmental organizations or nongovernmental organizations co-operating with the United Nations to protect and assist such a child and to trace the parents or other members of the family of any refugee child in order to obtain information necessary for reunification with his or her family. In cases where no parents or other members of the family can be found, the child shall be accorded the same protection as any other child permanently or temporarily deprived of his or her family environment for any reason, as set forth in the present Convention.

Article 23

1. States Parties recognize that a mentally or physically disabled child should enjoy a full and decent life, in conditions which ensure dignity, promote self-reliance and facilitate the child's active participation in the community.

2. States Parties recognize the right of the disabled child to special care and shall encourage and ensure the extension, subject to available resources, to the eligible child and those responsible for his or her care, of assistance for which application is made and which is appropriate to the child's condition and to the circumstances of the parents or others caring for the child.

3. Recognizing the special needs of a disabled child, assistance extended in accordance with paragraph 2 of the present article shall be provided free of charge, whenever possible, taking into account the financial resources of the parents or others caring for the child, and shall be designed to ensure that the disabled child has effective access to and receives education, training, health care services, rehabilitation services, preparation for employment and recreation opportunities in a manner conducive to the child's achieving the fullest possible social integration and individual development, including his or her cultural and spiritual development.

4. States Parties shall promote, in the spirit of international co-operation, the exchange of appropriate information in the field of preventive health care and of medical, psychological and

functional treatment of disabled children, including dissemination of and access to information concerning methods of rehabilitation, education and vocational services, with the aim of enabling States Parties to improve their capabilities and skills and to widen their experience in these areas. In this regard, particular account shall be taken of the needs of developing countries.

Article 24

1. States Parties recognize the right of the child to the enjoyment of the highest attainable standard of health and to facilities for the treatment of illness and rehabilitation of health. States Parties shall strive to ensure that no child is deprived of his or her right of access to such health care services.

2. States Parties shall pursue full implementation of this right and, in particular, shall take appropriate measures:

    (a) To diminish infant and child mortality;

    (b) To ensure the provision of necessary medical assistance and health care to all children with emphasis on the development of primary health care;

    (c) To combat disease and malnutrition, including within the framework of primary health care, through, inter alia, the application of readily available technology and through the provision of adequate nutritious foods and clean drinking-water, taking into consideration the dangers and risks of environmental pollution;

    (d) To ensure appropriate pre-natal and post-natal health care for mothers;

    (e) To ensure that all segments of society, in particular parents and children, are informed, have access to education and are supported in the use of basic knowledge of child health and nutrition, the advantages of breastfeeding, hygiene and environmental sanitation and the prevention of accidents;

    (f) To develop preventive health care, guidance for parents and family planning education and services.

3. States Parties shall take all effective and appropriate measures with a view to abolishing traditional practices prejudicial to the health of children.

4. States Parties undertake to promote and encourage international co-operation with a view to achieving progressively the full realization of the right recognized in the present article. In this regard, particular account shall be taken of the needs of developing countries.

Article 25

States Parties recognize the right of a child who has been placed by the competent authorities for the purposes of care, protection or treatment of his or her physical or mental health, to a periodic review of the treatment provided to the child and all other circumstances relevant to his or her placement.

Article 26

1. States Parties shall recognize for every child the right to benefit from social security, including social insurance, and shall take the necessary measures to achieve the full realization of this right in accordance with their national law.

2. The benefits should, where appropriate, be granted, taking into account the resources and the circumstances of the child and persons having responsibility for the maintenance of the child, as well as any other consideration relevant to an application for benefits made by or on behalf of the child.

Article 27

1. States Parties recognize the right of every child to a standard of living adequate for the child's physical, mental, spiritual, moral and social development.

2. The parent(s) or others responsible for the child have the primary responsibility to secure, within their abilities and financial capacities, the conditions of living necessary for the child's development.

3. States Parties, in accordance with national conditions and within their means, shall take appropriate measures to assist parents and others responsible for the child to implement this right and shall in case of need provide material assistance and support programmes, particularly with regard to nutrition, clothing and housing.

4. States Parties shall take all appropriate measures to secure the recovery of maintenance for the

child from the parents or other persons having financial responsibility for the child, both within the State Party and from abroad. In particular, where the person having financial responsibility for the child lives in a State different from that of the child, States Parties shall promote the accession to international agreements or the conclusion of such agreements, as well as the making of other appropriate arrangements.

Article 28

1. States Parties recognize the right of the child to education, and with a view to achieving this right progressively and on the basis of equal opportunity, they shall, in particular:

   (a) Make primary education compulsory and available free to all;

   (b) Encourage the development of different forms of secondary education, including general and vocational education, make them available and accessible to every child, and take appropriate measures such as the introduction of free education and offering financial assistance in case of need;

   (c) Make higher education accessible to all on the basis of capacity by every appropriate means;

   (d) Make educational and vocational information and guidance available and accessible to all children;

   (e) Take measures to encourage regular attendance at schools and the reduction of drop-out rates.

2. States Parties shall take all appropriate measures to ensure that school discipline is administered in a manner consistent with the child's human dignity and in conformity with the present Convention.

3. States Parties shall promote and encourage international co-operation in matters relating to education, in particular with a view to contributing to the elimination of ignorance and illiteracy throughout the world and facilitating access to scientific and technical knowledge and modern teaching methods. In this regard, particular account shall be taken of the needs of developing countries.

Article 29

1. States Parties agree that the education of the child shall be directed to:

   (a) The development of the child's personality, talents and mental and physical abilities to their fullest potential;

   (b) The development of respect for human rights and fundamental freedoms, and for the principles enshrined in the Charter of the United Nations;

   (c) The development of respect for the child's parents, his or her own cultural identity, language and values, for the national values of the country in which the child is living, the country from which he or she may originate, and for civilizations different from his or her own;

    (d) The preparation of the child for responsible life in a free society, in the spirit of understanding, peace, tolerance, equality of sexes, and friendship among all peoples, ethnic, national and religious groups and persons of indigenous origin;

    (e) The development of respect for the natural environment.

2. No part of the present article or article 28 shall be construed so as to interfere with the liberty of individuals and bodies to establish and direct educational institutions, subject always to the observance of the principle set forth in paragraph 1 of the present article and to the requirements that the education given in such institutions shall conform to such minimum standards as may be laid down by the State.

Article 30

In those States in which ethnic, religious or linguistic minorities or persons of indigenous origin exist, a child belonging to such a minority or who is indigenous shall not be denied the right, in community with other members of his or her group, to enjoy his or her own culture, to profess and practise his or her own religion, or to use his or her own language.

Article 31

1. States Parties recognize the right of the child to rest and leisure, to engage in play and recreational activities appropriate to the age of the child and to participate freely in cultural life and the arts.

2. States Parties shall respect and promote the right of the child to participate fully in cultural and artistic life and shall encourage the provision of appropriate and equal opportunities for cultural, artistic, recreational and leisure activity.

Article 32

1. States Parties recognize the right of the child to be protected from economic exploitation and from performing any work that is likely to be hazardous or to interfere with the child's education, or to be harmful to the child's health or physical, mental, spiritual, moral or social development.

2. States Parties shall take legislative, administrative, social and educational measures to ensure the implementation of the present article. To this end, and having regard to the relevant provisions of other international instruments, States Parties shall in particular:

   (a) Provide for a minimum age or minimum ages for admission to employment;

   (b) Provide for appropriate regulation of the hours and conditions of employment;

   (c) Provide for appropriate penalties or other sanctions to ensure the effective enforcement of the present article.

Article 33

States Parties shall take all appropriate measures, including legislative, administrative, social and educational measures, to protect children from the illicit use of narcotic drugs and psychotropic substances as defined in the relevant international treaties, and to prevent the use of children in the illicit production and trafficking of such substances.

Article 34

States Parties undertake to protect the child from all forms of sexual exploitation and sexual abuse. For these purposes, States Parties shall in particular take all appropriate national, bilateral and multilateral measures to prevent:

(a)   The inducement or coercion of a child to engage in any unlawful sexual activity;

(b)   The exploitative use of children in prostitution or other unlawful sexual practices;

(c)   The exploitative use of children in pornographic performances and materials.

Article 35

States Parties shall take all appropriate national, bilateral and multilateral measures to prevent the abduction of, the sale of or traffic in children for any purpose or in any form.

Article 36

States Parties shall protect the child against all other forms of exploitation prejudicial to any aspects of the child's welfare.

Article 37

States Parties shall ensure that:

(a) No child shall be subjected to torture or other cruel, inhuman or degrading treatment or punishment. Neither capital punishment nor life imprisonment without possibility of release shall be imposed for offences committed by persons below eighteen years of age;

(b) No child shall be deprived of his or her liberty unlawfully or arbitrarily. The arrest, detention or imprisonment of a child shall be in conformity with the law and shall be used only as a measure of last resort and for the shortest appropriate period of time;

(c) Every child deprived of liberty shall be treated with humanity and respect for the inherent dignity of the human person, and in a manner which takes into account the needs of persons of his or her age. In particular, every child deprived of liberty shall be separated from adults unless it is considered in the child's best interest not to do so and shall have the right to maintain contact with his or her family through correspondence and visits, save in exceptional circumstances;

(d) Every child deprived of his or her liberty shall have the right to prompt access to legal and other appropriate assistance, as well as the right to challenge the legality of the deprivation of his or her liberty before a court or other competent, independent and impartial authority, and to a prompt decision on any such action.

Article 38

1. States Parties undertake to respect and to ensure respect for rules of international humanitarian law applicable to them in armed conflicts which are relevant to the child.

2. States Parties shall take all feasible measures to ensure that persons who have not attained the age of fifteen years do not take a direct part in hostilities.

3. States Parties shall refrain from recruiting any person who has not attained the age of fifteen years into their armed forces. In recruiting among those persons who have attained the age of fifteen years but who have not attained the age of eighteen years, States Parties shall endeavour to give priority to those who are oldest.

4. In accordance with their obligations under international humanitarian law to protect the civilian population in armed conflicts, States Parties shall take all feasible measures to ensure protection and care of children who are affected by an armed conflict.

Article 39

States Parties shall take all appropriate measures to promote physical and psychological recovery and social reintegration of a child victim of: any form of neglect, exploitation, or abuse; torture or any other form of cruel, inhuman or degrading treatment or punishment; or armed conflicts. Such recovery and reintegration shall take place in an environment which fosters the health, self-respect and dignity of the child.

Article 40

1. States Parties recognize the right of every child alleged as, accused of, or recognized as having infringed the penal law to be treated in a manner consistent with the promotion of the child's sense of dignity and worth, which reinforces the child's respect for the human rights and fundamental freedoms of others and which takes into account the child's age and the desirability of promoting the child's reintegration and the child's assuming a constructive role in society.

2. To this end, and having regard to the relevant provisions of international instruments, States Parties shall, in particular, ensure that:

   (a) No child shall be alleged as, be accused of, or recognized as having infringed the penal law by reason of acts or omissions that were not prohibited by national or international law at the time they were committed;

   (b) Every child alleged as or accused of having infringed the penal law has at least the following guarantees:

      (i) To be presumed innocent until proven guilty according to law;

      (ii) To be informed promptly and directly of the charges against him or her, and, if appropriate, through his or her parents or legal guardians, and to have legal or other appropriate assistance in the preparation and presentation of his or her defence;

    (iii) To have the matter determined without delay by a competent, independent and impartial authority or judicial body in a fair hearing according to law, in the presence of legal or other appropriate assistance and, unless it is considered not to be in the best interest of the child, in particular, taking into account his or her age or situation, his or her parents or legal guardians;

    (iv) Not to be compelled to give testimony or to confess guilt; to examine or have examined adverse witnesses and to obtain the participation and examination of witnesses on his or her behalf under conditions of equality;

    (v) If considered to have infringed the penal law, to have this decision and any measures imposed in consequence thereof reviewed by a higher competent, independent and impartial authority or judicial body according to law;

    (vi) To have the free assistance of an interpreter if the child cannot understand or speak the language used;

    (vii) To have his or her privacy fully respected at all stages of the proceedings.

3. States Parties shall seek to promote the establishment of laws, procedures, authorities and institutions specifically applicable to children alleged as, accused of, or recognized as having infringed the penal law, and, in particular:

(a) The establishment of a minimum age below which children shall be presumed not to have the capacity to infringe the penal law;

(b) Whenever appropriate and desirable, measures for dealing with such children without resorting to judicial proceedings, providing that human rights and legal safeguards are fully respected.

4. A variety of dispositions, such as care, guidance and supervision orders; counselling; probation; foster care; education and vocational training programmes and other alternatives to institutional care shall be available to ensure that children are dealt with in a manner appropriate to their well-being and proportionate both to their circumstances and the offence.

Article 41

Nothing in the present Convention shall affect any provisions which are more conducive to the realization of the rights of the child and which may be contained in:

(a) The law of a State Party; or

(b) International law in force for that State.

Part II

Article 42

States Parties undertake to make the principles and provisions of the Convention widely known, by appropriate and active means, to adults and children alike.

Article 43

1. For the purpose of examining the progress made by States Parties in achieving the realization of the obligations undertaken in the present Convention, there shall be established a Committee on the Rights of the Child, which shall carry out the functions hereinafter provided.

2. The Committee shall consist of eighteen experts of high moral standing and recognized competence in the field covered by this Convention. The members of the Committee shall be elected by States Parties from among their nationals and shall serve in their personal capacity, consideration being given to equitable geographical distribution, as well as to the principal legal systems.

3. The members of the Committee shall be elected by secret ballot from a list of persons nominated by States Parties. Each State Party may nominate one person from among its own nationals.

4. The initial election to the Committee shall be held no later than six months after the date of the entry into force of the present Convention and thereafter every second year. At least four months before the date of each election, the Secretary-General of the United Nations shall address a letter to States Parties inviting them to submit their nominations within two months. The Secretary-General shall subsequently prepare a list in alphabetical order of all persons thus nominated, indicating States Parties which have nominated them, and shall submit it to the States Parties to the present Convention.

5. The elections shall be held at meetings of States Parties convened by the Secretary-General at United Nations Headquarters. At those meetings, for which two thirds of States Parties shall constitute a quorum, the persons elected to the Committee shall be those who obtain the largest number of votes and an absolute majority of the votes of the representatives of States Parties present and voting.

6. The members of the Committee shall be elected for a term of four years. They shall be eligible for re-election if renominated. The term of five of the members elected at the first election shall expire at the end of two years; immediately after the first election, the names of these five members shall be chosen by lot by the Chairman of the meeting.

7. If a member of the Committee dies or resigns or declares that for any other cause he or she can no longer perform the duties of the Committee, the State Party which nominated the member shall appoint another expert from among its nationals to serve for the remainder of the term, subject to the approval of the Committee.

8. The Committee shall establish its own rules of procedure.

9. The Committee shall elect its officers for a period of two years.

10. The meetings of the Committee shall normally be held at United Nations Headquarters or at any other convenient place as determined by the Committee. The Committee shall normally meet

annually. The duration of the meetings of the Committee shall be determined, and reviewed, if necessary, by a meeting of the States Parties to the present Convention, subject to the approval of the General Assembly.

11. The Secretary-General of the United Nations shall provide the necessary staff and facilities for the effective performance of the functions of the Committee under the present Convention.

12. With the approval of the General Assembly, the members of the Committee established under the present Convention shall receive emoluments from United Nations resources on such terms and conditions as the Assembly may decide.

Article 44

1. States Parties undertake to submit to the Committee, through the Secretary-General of the United Nations, reports on the measures they have adopted which give effect to the rights recognized herein and on the progress made on the enjoyment of those rights

    (a) Within two years of the entry into force of the Convention for the State Party concerned;

    (b) Thereafter every five years.

2. Reports made under the present article shall indicate factors and difficulties, if any, affecting the degree of fulfilment of the obligations under the present Convention. Reports shall also contain sufficient information to provide the Committee with a comprehensive understanding of the

implementation of the Convention in the country concerned.

3. A State Party which has submitted a comprehensive initial report to the Committee need not, in its subsequent reports submitted in accordance with paragraph 1 (b) of the present article, repeat basic information previously provided.

4. The Committee may request from States Parties further information relevant to the implementation of the Convention.

5. The Committee shall submit to the General Assembly, through the Economic and Social Council, every two years, reports on its activities.

6. States Parties shall make their reports widely available to the public in their own countries.

Article 45

In order to foster the effective implementation of the Convention and to encourage international co-operation in the field covered by the Convention:

(a) The specialized agencies, the United Nations Children's Fund, and other United Nations organs shall be entitled to be represented at the consideration of the implementation of such provisions of the present Convention as fall within the scope of their mandate. The Committee may invite the specialized agencies, the United Nations Children's Fund and other competent bodies as it may consider appropriate to provide expert advice on the implementation of the Convention in areas falling within the scope of their respective mandates. The Committee may invite the specialized agencies, the United Nations Children's Fund, and other United Nations organs to submit reports on the implementation of the Convention in areas falling within the scope of their activities;

(b) The Committee shall transmit, as it may consider appropriate, to the specialized agencies, the United Nations Children's Fund and other competent bodies, any reports from States Parties that contain a request, or indicate a need, for technical advice or assistance, along with the Committee's observations and suggestions, if any, on these requests or indications;

(c) The Committee may recommend to the General Assembly to request the Secretary-General to undertake on its behalf studies on specific issues relating to the rights of the child;

(d) The Committee may make suggestions and general recommendations based on information received pursuant to articles 44 and 45 of the present Convention. Such suggestions and general recommendations shall be transmitted to any State Party concerned and reported to the General Assembly, together with comments, if any, from States Parties.

Part III

Article 46

The present Convention shall be open for signature by all States.

Article 47

The present Convention is subject to ratification. Instruments of ratification shall be deposited with the Secretary-General of the United Nations.

Article 48

The present Convention shall remain open for accession by any State. The instruments of accession shall be deposited with the Secretary-General of the United Nations.

Article 49

1. The present Convention shall enter into force on the thirtieth day following the date of deposit with the Secretary-General of the United Nations of the twentieth instrument of ratification or accession.

2. For each State ratifying or acceding to the Convention after the deposit of the twentieth instrument of ratification or accession, the Convention shall enter into force on the thirtieth day after the deposit by such State of its instrument of ratification or accession.

Article 50

1. Any State Party may propose an amendment and file it with the Secretary-General of the United Nations. The Secretary-General shall thereupon communicate the proposed amendment to States Parties, with a request that they indicate whether they favour a conference of States Parties for the purpose of considering and voting upon the

proposals. In the event that, within four months from the date of such communication, at least one third of the States Parties favour such a conference, the Secretary-General shall convene the conference under the auspices of the United Nations. Any amendment adopted by a majority of States Parties present and voting at the conference shall be submitted to the General Assembly for approval.

2. An amendment adopted in accordance with paragraph 1 of the present article shall enter into force when it has been approved by the General Assembly of the United Nations and accepted by a two thirds majority of States Parties.

3. When an amendment enters into force, it shall be binding on those States Parties which have accepted it, other States Parties still being bound by the provisions of the present Convention and any earlier amendments which they have accepted.

Article 51

1. The Secretary-General of the United Nations shall receive and circulate to all States the text of reservations made by States at the time of ratification or accession.

2. A reservation incompatible with the object and purpose of the present Convention shall not be permitted.

3. Reservations may be withdrawn at any time by notification to that effect addressed to the Secretary-General of the United Nations, who

shall then inform all States. Such notification shall take effect on the date on which it is received by the Secretary-General.

Article 52

A State Party may denounce the present Convention by written notification to the Secretary-General of the United Nations. Denunciation becomes effective one year after the date of receipt of the notification by the Secretary-General.

Article 53

The Secretary-General of the United Nations is designated as the depositary of the present Convention.

Article 54

The original of the present Convention, of which the Arabic, Chinese, English, French, Russian and Spanish texts are equally authentic, shall be deposited with the Secretary-General of the United Nations. IN WITNESS THEREOF the undersigned plenipotentiaries, being duly authorized thereto by their respective governments, have signed the present Convention.

APPENDIX 2

List of identifying issues in a child's life that may place them at greater risk of abuse or neglect

(as included in Children First Guidance 2017)

Parent or carer factors:
- Drug and alcohol misuse
- Addiction, including gambling
- Mental health issues
- Parental disability issues, including learning or intellectual disability
- Conflictual relationships
- Domestic violence
- Adolescent parents

Child factors:
- Age
- Gender
- Sexuality
- Disability
- Mental health issues, including self-harm and suicide
- Communication difficulties

- Trafficked/Exploited
- Previous abuse
- Young carer

Community factors:

- Cultural, ethnic, religious or faith-based norms in the family or community which may not meet the standards of child welfare or protection required in this jurisdiction
- Culture-specific practices, including:
  - Female genital mutilation
  - Forced marriage
  - Honour-based violence
  - Radicalisation

Environmental factors:

- Housing issues
- Children who are out of home and not living with their parents, whether temporarily or permanently
- Poverty/Begging
- Bullying
- Internet and social media-related concerns

Poor motivation or willingness of parents/guardians to engage:

- Non-attendance at appointments
- Lack of insight or understanding of how the child is being affected

- Lack of understanding about what needs to happen to bring about change
- Avoidance of contact and reluctance to work with services
- Inability or unwillingness to comply with agreed plans

APPENDIX 3

Tusla standard reporting form to report abuse

(in line with Children First Guidance 2017)

TÚSLA An Ghníomhaireacht um Leanaí agus an Teaghlach
Child and Family Agency

Child Protection and Welfare Report Form

MANDATED PERSONS AND NON MANDATED PERSONS
(Children First Act 2015 & Children First National Guidance)

Use block letters when filling out this form.
Fields marked with an * are mandatory.

1. Tusla Area (this is where the child resides)*	

2. Date of Report*	

3. Details of Child

First Name*		Surname*	
Male*	☐	Female*	☐
Address*		Date of Birth*	
		Estimated Age*	
		School Name	
		School Address	
Eircode			

4. Details of Concerns*

Please complete the following section with as much detail about the specific child protection or welfare concern or allegation as possible. Include dates, times, incident details and names of anyone who observed any incident. Please include the parents and child's view, if known. Please attach additional sheets, if necessary

Please see *'Tusla Children First – A Guide for the Reporting of Child Protection and Welfare Concerns'* for additional assistance on the steps to consider in making a report to Tusla

5. Type of Concern

Child Welfare Concern	☐		
Emotional Abuse	☐	Physical Abuse	☐
Neglect	☐	Sexual Abuse	☐

6. Details of Reporter

First Name		Surname	
Address If reporting in a professional capacity, please use your professional address		Organisation	
		Position Held	
		Mobile No.	
		Telephone No.	
Eircode		Email Address	

TÚSLA An Ghníomhaireacht um Leanaí agus an Teaghlach
Child and Family Agency

Child Protection and Welfare Report Form

MANDATED PERSONS AND NON MANDATED PERSONS
(Children First Act 2015 & Children First National Guidance)

Is this a Mandated Report made under Sec 14, Children First Act 2015?*	Yes	☐	No	☐
Mandated Person's Type				

7. Details of Other Persons Where a Joint Report is Being Made

First Name		Surname	
Address If reporting in a professional capacity, please use your professional address		Organisation	
		Position Held	
		Mobile No.	
		Telephone No.	
Eircode		Email Address	

First Name		Surname	
Address If reporting in a professional capacity, please use your professional address		Organisation	
		Position Held	
		Mobile No.	
		Telephone No.	
Eircode		Email Address	

8. Parents Aware of Report

Are the child's parents/carers aware that this concern is being reported to Tusla?*	Yes	☐	No	☐
If the parent/carer does not know, please indicate reasons:				

9. Relationships

Details of Mother

First Name		Surname	
Address		Mobile No.	
		Telephone No.	
		Email Address	
Eircode			

Is the Mother a Legal Guardian?*	Yes	☐	No	☐

Details of Father

First Name		Surname	
Address		Mobile No.	
		Telephone No.	
		Email Address	
Eircode			

TÚSLA An Ghníomhaireacht um Leanaí agus an Teaghlach Child and Family Agency

Child Protection and Welfare Report Form

MANDATED PERSONS AND NON MANDATED PERSONS
(Children First Act 2015 & Children First National Guidance)

Is the Father a Legal Guardian?*		Yes	☐	No	☐

10. Household Composition

First Name	Surname	Relationship	Date of Birth	Estimated Age	Additional Information e.g. school, occupation, other

11. Details of Person(s) Allegedly Causing Harm

First Name*		Surname*	
Male*	☐	Female*	☐
Address		Date of Birth	
		Estimated Age	
		Mobile No.	
		Telephone No.	
Eircode		Email Address	
Occupation		Organisation	
Position Held			

Relationship to Child	
Address at time of alleged incident	
If name unknown please indicate reason	

First Name*		Surname*	
Male*	☐	Female*	☐
Address		Date of Birth	
		Estimated Age	
		Mobile No.	
		Telephone No.	
Eircode		Email Address	
Occupation		Organisation	
Position Held			

Relationship to Child	
Address at time of alleged incident	
If name unknown please indicate reason	

TÜSLA
An Ghníomhaireacht um
Leanaí agus an Teaghlach
Child and Family Agency

Child Protection and Welfare Report Form

MANDATED PERSONS AND NON MANDATED PERSONS
(Children First Act 2015 & Children First National Guidance)

12. Name and Address of Other Organisations, Personnel or Agencies Known to be Involved Currently or Previously with the Family

Profession	First Name	Surname	Address	Contact Number	Recent Contact e.g. 3/6/9 months ago
Social Worker					
Public Health Nurse					
GP					
Hospital					
School					
Gardaí					
Pre-school/ crèche					
Other					

13. Any Other Relevant Information, Including any Previous Contact with the Child or Family

Please ensure you have indicated if this is a mandated report in section 6.
Thank you for completing the report form.

In completing this report form you are providing details on yourself and on others. Details such as name, address and date of birth fall under the definition of 'Personal Data' in the Data Protection Acts, 1988 & 2003. Tusla has a responsibility under these Acts in its capacity as a Data Controller to, amongst other things, obtain and process this data fairly; keep it safe and secure; and to keep it for a specified lawful purpose. That purpose is to fulfil our statutory responsibility under the Child Care Act 1991 to promote the protection and welfare of children. Tusla may, during the course of the assessment of this report disclose such Personal Data to other agencies including An Garda Síochána. Further details about Tusla's responsibilities as a Data Controller and your rights as a Data Subject can be found on our website, www.tusla.ie. As you are providing Personal Data on others, you are a Data Processor. We ask that you only provide those details that are necessary for the report and that you keep this report and the Personal Data contained in it secure from unauthorised access, disclosure, destruction or accidental loss.

14. For Completion by Tusla Authorised Person on Receipt of Report

Report Received by					
First Name		Surname		Date	

Mandated Report Acknowledgement by

TÚSLA An Ghníomhaireacht um Leanaí agus an Teaghlach Child and Family Agency

Child Protection and Welfare Report Form

MANDATED PERSONS AND NON MANDATED PERSONS
(Children First Act 2015 & Children First National Guidance)

First Name		Surname		Date Sent	

Authorised Person Signature*	
Date*	

Child Previously Known		Yes	☐	No	☐
Allocated Case No					

GLOSSARY

A mensa et thoro   A Latin phrase that literally translates as 'from board and bed'. When used in a divorce context it means that the couple do not live together. This expression is an old one and the equivalent in modern terminology is 'being separated'.

Anomaly   Something that is different from what is expected.

Antecedent rights   Rights that are already in existence.

Article   A clause in an agreement or document.

Capacity   The ability or power to do something or a person's legal competence.

Care Contract   The level of trust that is involved in a caring position such as childcare or teaching. It entails a commitment to providing care in place of someone else or indeed along with somebody else where everybody has a role in the care that is provided.

Common Good This expression is found throughout the Irish Constitution and means that some individual rights are limited so as not to interfere unnecessarily with other people's needs and rights. In other words, a balance is required, and this may restrict the application of some of our rights so that we can all live together equally as a society.

Constitution Most countries have a written constitution that sets out the rules and procedures by which that country and individuals in that country are governed and the method by which its laws are drawn up.

Contemporaneous Contemporaneous notes are those made at that moment in time, i.e. they are made at the moment that the action you are recording is taking place. They would usually be dated and in a diary format as they are written on a regular basis as you go along.

Convention   A written agreement, usually of an international nature, which is adopted by states to govern whatever is covered by the convention.

Guardian *ad litem*   Somebody appointed to look after the best interests of the child and to read and inform themselves of the facts on behalf of the child and to give an objective opinion to the judge on what would be in the best interests of that child.

Imprescriptible rights   Rights that exist whether you use them or not – they cannot be ignored.

Inalienable rights   Rights that cannot be removed, transferred or altered.

In loco parentis   A person acting in place of parents on behalf of a child or dependent person.

Laws   The rules that are written down as acts of government, such as the Child Care Act 1991.

Legally binding   Something that has legal protection and cannot be changed without getting court approval.

Legislation
All or part of a the written law of a country. Usually in Ireland this relates to acts of government, an example of which would be the Child Care Act 1991.

Preamble
An introductory statement that usually explains the intentions of what is to be presented.

Protocol
The accepted code of behaviour or action in relation to a certain thing or situation that might arise.

Ratified
Where an agreement, treaty, convention or some other agreement is signed as having effect.

Referendum
The name given to the voting process that is used in relation to proposed changes to the Constitution. The Irish Constitution states that a person who is registered to vote essentially has the right to vote in a referendum.

Repatriation
Sending somebody back to their country of origin.

INDEX